GAELIC – A PAST & FUTURE PROSPECT

GAELIC –
a PAST and FUTURE PROSPECT

Kenneth MacKinnon

SALTIRE

Printed and bound in Britain by Billings and Sons Ltd, Worcester.
Cover printed by A4 Print, Inverness.

Design by Sarah Fraser, Balnain.

The publisher acknowledges subsidy from the Scottish Arts Council towards the publication of this volume.

Published in 1991
by the Saltire Society,
9 Fountain Close,
High Street,
Edinburgh EH1 1TF

British Library Cataloguing in Publication Data:
MacKinnon, Kenneth

    Gaelic: past,present and future prospect

    1. Scottish Gaelic language

    I. Title

    491.63

ISBN 0-85411-047-X

CONTENTS

INTRODUCTION

A CONSTANT GROUND

What is the relevance of the Gaelic language in Scotland today?

Is there any general public image of its place in the story of the Scottish people – or any sense of its significance in everyday modern life? In the history books it is too often little more than a footnote if it is anything at all – in modern life perhaps an anachronism. For the mass, if they are watching the right channel at the right time it is a peculiarity on the fringe of national life and pretty much for the fringe alone.

And yet there is a sense in which the Gaelic language is a part of the personal identity and everyday life of almost every Scot. More than that, the language is at the root of the very entity of what came to be called Scotland – indeed the very reason why it is recognised as such and called Scotland today: the

land of the Scots, the Gaelic-speaking people who
came over the sea from eastern Ulster, and established their kingdom and their language throughout
what we now know as Scotland and even beyond.
That is why, even today, there are few Scots who do
not bear either a surname or a forename of Gaelic
origin, or who do not live, work or travel past places
every day whose names go back to that language.

Lowland Scottish speech itself originated in the
contact between Angles and other incomers and the
Celtic peoples who were here already. Of Anglo-Cel-
tic rather than Anglo-Saxon in origin, it is still readily
distinguishable from the Standard English of today.
In these and many other ways, Gaelic lives today
upon the lips of all Scots whether or not they realise it
or whether or not their education or the media enable
them to recognise it.

The continuing and living culture handed on to us
through the Gaelic language has important implications not only within Scotland but also far beyond.
The continuity of Gaelic extends unbroken from its
origins in Ireland, throughout Scotland's history, and
today beyond Scotland's borders wherever the
descendants of the Gaels have spread and settled. Of
all Scotland's distinctive institutions, it is this language
and the culture which derives from it, which most
effectively defines an ethnic identity for the Scots as a
people at home and abroad. It is tragic that so early in
Scotland's modern history English replaced Gaelic as
the language of the majority of her people. Nevertheless, this essentially Gaelic character underlies much
of what is distinctive in Scottish national life. The
national costume originated in Gaelic dress. The
national drink is Gaelic in name. Both the Scots Lang-

uage and Scottish English show influences of Gaelic as the original language of the Scots. For in all these ways, Gaelic is woven into the fabric of Scottish history and society as the red or green ground underlying the setts of the many individual tartans, or the *ùrlar* (vein) running through all the variations of the *piobaireachd* of Scottish history. It is that constant ground underlying the whole of Scotland's story. Remove it and its influence and Scotland is merely North Britain.

Gaelic is seen in the modern myth as surviving as the everyday language of a handful of hardy crofters and fisherfolk battling out a marginal existence in a remote if romantic corner of the country. Nothing particularly central to the life of the nation – and no special measures are necessary since the Gaels are now virtually all bilingual anyway. No civil rights issues, no problems in making yourself understood, and no ethnic minority complications. So there is nothing much to worry about – nothing like the fuss in Wales, where the language is significant throughout the country. Romanticised and tartanised, Gaeldom's symbols decorate shortbread tins. Devoid of its people, the landscape of Gaeldom features on calendars and Christmas cards.

The reality is that Gaelic is spoken throughout Scotland today. There are moreover almost as many Gaelic speakers in the Lowlands as the Highlands, and almost as many in the cities as in the islands. A century ago the Highland counties contained over three-quarters of all Gaelic speakers, but in 1981 this area had shrunk to under 60%. In fact, the vast majority of Gaelic-speakers do not live in 'Gaelic-speaking areas' at all. By 1981, the truly Gaelic areas

where over three-quarters of the population speak
Gaelic contained only one in four of all Gaelic
speakers, the others being encountered just about
anywhere else you were likely to go. And although
the crofting community continues to encapsulate the
core of Gaeldom, modern crofting of necessity entails
a life-style capable of combining with any other occupation of the modern world.

The miniscule size of the Gaelic community – there
are around 80,000 speakers of the language today –
might indicate a language which is very rapidly on the
way out. Decline there has been – from around a
quarter of a million a century ago – but the 1971 and
1981 censuses witnessed an arrest of this decline, with
some encouraging growth-points. Numbers were
down to 80,978 in 1961, but ten years later had
climbed back to 88,892 (an increase of almost 10%).
Although numbers fell back to around their 1961
level in 1981 (79,307 speakers of Gaelic, 82,620 with
speaking, reading and writing abilities), for the first
time ever numbers and proportions of Gaelic
speakers increased in the principal Gaelic areas of the
Western Isles and parts of Skye. Another encouraging feature was the growth of Gaelic abilities amongst
young people in those areas where there had been
Gaelic teaching schemes in the schools, and where
there was work for their parents. There is a success
story here and a lesson for the language.

Today there is a thrusting new spirit concerning
the language which says that despite the putting
down of the language in the past, and despite the
decades of neglect, it has survived and its recovery
will be regained. Recent years have seen an upsurge
of interest in the language in Scotland and beyond.

The nationwide dimension of Gaelic reminds us that the language is an essential and defining aspect of Scotland's heritage. Perhaps the next step is to secure proper official recognition and its rightful place in the national culture. If it is merely seen as relevant only in the ever-decreasing 'Gaelic-speaking area' of the far northwest, its doom is sealed. If it is recognised as part of the living heritage of all Scots, it is a language with its part to play in a Scottish future.

Gaelic life and culture have a message for the world. The continuing story of the Gaelic people is a story of adaptation in the face of adversity. But they have not always been in retreat. Their present homelands were actually retaken from the Norsemen in the early middle ages, and with the decline of Viking seapower, the Gaels replaced them. The seafaring tradition continues strongly today.

Gaelic culture has been influential in the wider world. Gaelic speakers brought the Christian faith, literacy and humane learning to their pagan neighbours in the days of the Celtic Church, ending the Dark Ages in the northern Anglo-Saxon kingdoms. The Irish scholar Alice Green regarded them as having 'taught the English the letters they still use'. The influence of this church of the Gaels extended as far afield as northern Italy and Kiev and, in Lord Clark's words, saved civilisation 'by the skin of its teeth.' Its language was by the 11th century the principal *lingua franca* of Scotland. Throughout subsequent centuries we note the Bruces urging Scotland and Ireland to common cause as the Scots and the Irish shared a common origin and 'spoke the same language'. Gaelic was the language used at the Parliament which Bruce convened at Ardchattan. Poets, historians and other writers in Lowland Scotland up until the 16th century readily acknowledged Gaelic to be the true and original Scottish language. For Walter Kennedy, *'it suld be al trew Scottis mennis lede.'* (*'Flyting with Dunbar'* c. 1500).

In later ages Gaelic transmuted a rich folklore into a high culture – and back again. Following the breaking-up of Gaelic society, Gaels went forth to colonise new lands, settle new countries and to carry their faith and their culture to distant parts of the world and play their part in the founding of new nations. And within their homeland time and time again, the Gaelic people have adapted to changing circumstance. The collapse of the independent Lordship of the Isles was followed by the formation of the clan system so often romanticised today. With the suppression of the bardic schools and the severance of the link with Gaelic Ireland during the 17th century, Scottish Gaelic culture was thrown back upon its own resources. In the 18th century the conflict on three continents of England and France used Scottish Gaels, North American Indians and the peoples of South Asia as pawns in world politics. The aftermath was the destruction of the clan system, forced migration, and recruitment for cannon-fodder in Britain's imperial wars. The Clearances, which followed in the 19th Century as capitalism 'improved' the Highlands, swept away the last remnants of traditional local autonomy and created a vast desert of sheep-runs, deer forests and grouse moors out of the homeland of the Gaels.

Yet time and time again they rallied. The political power of Gaeldom was destroyed: the Gaels rewove their traditions and their spiritual life. Their high culture was suppressed: the Gaels transformed their learned traditions into a popular culture. The clans were destroyed: a New Scotland was established overseas. New lairds attempted to place their own nominees in spiritual authority over the people; the people repudiated the false shepherds and flocked to their own. Through the Gaelic message of a spiritually awakened people, the Gaelic cause in secular and political life established a measure of security for the Gaelic people within their own homeland and they evolved a new social order: the crofting community.

Gaeldom today faces new challenges. Migration has continued to take its toll of the young and the innovative, and they have been encouraged to seek their careers outwith the home community, only to find their subsequent return economically daunting. New forms of economic activity in the *Gàidhealtachd* have always been associated with the intrusion of English. Education, the mass- media and administration have typically in the past been controlled from the outside and gave little heed to the local language. Modern transport systems have separated island from island, glen from glen: its patterns are laid down for easy interpenetration from the outside rather than for internal convenience, thus connecting the divided parts of the *Gàidhealtachd* to different outside centres. Although tourism, forestry, and extractive industries have threatened Gaeldom because their direction has been from the outside, the Gaels have used them to make some security for themselves and their way of life. Today there is a new willingness to use modern technology to work for the interests of Gaeldom, and to enable young people to have the means to use the benefits of new techniques and higher education within their own communities: to establish new enterprises and new forms of communication. Gaelic is no longer just the language of the loom and the spinning-wheel, but the language of the word-processor, the computer and the video.

In all this there exists the latent possibility of further transformations of Gaelic society. The mistake of development policy in the 1960s and '70s with the establishment of the Highlands and Islands Development Board was in attempting to bring the Highlands into the Industrial Revolution, which was regarded as a good thing and one which had largely bypassed the region. A policy of establishing 'growth-poles' was envisaged as providing the focal points for economic stimulus in their hinterlands. Large-scale industries were extended or established in Caithness, Lochaber and around the Moray Firth: nuclear power generation, aluminium smelting, pulp-milling, rig- fabrication. There were further prospects of oil-refining and petro-chemical industries based on them. These last never came, for by the 1980s the policy was conspicuously failing. Smelters and fabrication-yards closed, and even the prospects of the nuclear industries post-Chernobyl looked decidedly shaky. Nuclear waste dumping was then floated as their replacement.

The fact that the Industrial Revolution did not fully transform the Highlands and Islands is now very much an advantage in a 'post-industrial society' (or more properly a 'post-first-industrial-revolution society'). For the relatively pollution-free environment provides an opportunity for new manufactures which require high levels of purity and freedom from contamination. And the crofting system could readily form the basis of an alternative local economy utilising the energy-rich environment for sustainable new combinations of manufacturing and food-production.

Basically what stands in the way of that is that the necessary research and development have not yet been done. In many respects though the local economy is 'post- industrial' already – and this is for once to its advantage, if only it can be realised. 'Conservation' has sometimes been falsely contrasted with crofting – as if corncrakes and crofters had not co-existed in Uist for centuries, or in some way opposed to local employment – as if a multinational whisky company could not easily have dug its peat without disturbing white-fronted geese in Islay. Exploitation by outsiders has not generally produced stable local economies anyway. A sustainable local economy is not so much a *conservationist* as an *ecologically sound* economy – and such economies will sustain both crofters and corncrakes.

Such concerns are relevant to what this book is principally about. Its central problem is to explain how the original language of the Scots failed to become their national language of today, and why Gaelic is not referred to as Scots or Scottish in the same way that the Gaelic language of Ireland is called Irish by speakers of English. The historical process and the manipulation of ideas are very much bound up with the exercise of power and economic domination, as indeed is the language used to legitimate such processes and the languages spoken by the people involved in them.

This book is also intended as a discussion of the

problems of the present-day Gaelic community and to raise issues concerning its future. This book is therefore not a history of Gaelic literature, nor is it an account of the historical development of Gaelic as a language. Others have concerned themselves with these matters, and the bibliography directs the interested reader to studies in these fields. Literature and linguistics are closely linked to social processes – and indeed they cannot fully be understood unless they are related to the social history and historical sociology of the speech-community. This book is a first attempt at the social history and sociology of the language. And above all, it is concerned to apply these considerations in arguing a case for the retention of Gaelic in the Scotland of the future, and to suggest strategies which might assist this objective.

My concern in this is not that Gaelic should be 'preserved' or 'revived', but for it to flourish. Neither am I concerned with arguments about ideas of racial, linguistic or national 'purity'. I am much more interested in the study of a culture which has maintained itself and persisted in association with one of Europe's oldest literary languages, throughout centuries of persecution, neglect, denial of rights, extermination and clearance of its speakers, social and geographical disadvantages, and yet has survived to the present day. If Gaelic has been a 'dying' language, it has tenaciously resisted its oppressors. Gaelic and its culture have responded to their circumstances in development and adaptation. The language and its culture have given me much pleasure and delight. I have no wish to see them pass away in my lifetime or my grandchildren's. Rather I would wish to see them gain new life and flourish.

There are some who equate an interest in Gaelic culture with nostalgia, antiquarianism and narrow nationalism. 'It is an attempt to put back the clock.' (Although we should do just that if the clock is wrong.) I believe that Gaelic and its associated way of life, its literature, its social institutions and the values of its speakers spell out a story of adaption to change and autonomous development which have an important message for mankind. In this lies the distinctive Gaelic character whose heritage has value and relevance for the future. The conclusion of the book is a personal view of the ways in which the language and its culture are relevant to our present circumstances, of value to the world community and of importance for the future.

An Tòisigheachd, An t-Eilean Dubh, An Dàmhair, 1990
Ferintosh, The Black Isle, October 1990.

PART 1:
ORIGINS –
THE LION'S TONGUE

THE COMING
OF THE SCOTS

Child to parent, child to parent over some fifty or sixty generations from the Scots of today would bring us back to an Irish tribe, the Féni, whose kingdom of Dalriada in Northern Ireland started to expand into the Western Highlands and Islands from about 200 A.D. onwards. In time these settlers – the *'Scotti'* from 'Scotia' – Ireland – came to outnumber their fellow countrymen of Ulster and their kings from the days of Fergus Mór mac Erc from about 500 A.D. onwards ruled from Argyll *(Oirthir Gháidheal* – the Coast of the Gaels), and from this base this people came to give their name and their language to Northern Britain. The Kingdom of the Scots is now merged in the British State, and in 1981 Gaelic was spoken by some 80,000 only of the Scots. Yet the story of this community and its culture is a continuing one. It is not, as yet, 'ane end of ane auld sang'.

As a way of life the culture of the early Scottish kingdom was probably little distinguished from that of other peoples of Dark Age Britain. However, they were probably better organised socially and militarily, as one of their surviving chronicles the Senchus Fer nAlban seems to indicate. Also from the point of view of ideas, values and ideologies these people were the first in post-Roman Britain to take up Christianity and the corpus of learning associated with it. Thus we may claim for their language, after the languages of classical Greece and Rome, to be the oldest living literary language of Europe.

It was Columba – *Calum Cille* – who brought Christianity to the Scots of Alba and the Picts of Caledonia and established humane learning in these parts of Britain. From 563 A.D. onwards, from his base in Iona, Columba's activity extended to convert first the Scots, then the Picts, the kingdoms to the south, those of northern, eastern and midland England and further afield throughout central and eastern Europe. The Columban church developed a high culture whose remains we can see today in magnificent illuminated manuscript books such as the *Book of Kells*, believed to have been made in Iona, and the Lindisfarne Gospels, as well as in marvellously carved crosses, reliquaries and metalwork. On the less material side, intense missionary zeal brought Christian values, literacy and learning to peoples such as the Anglo-Saxons as far south as London and even Sussex.

In Northern Britain at this time four ethnically distinguishable peoples occupied the land: the Scots themselves, Gaelic in speech and Irish in origin, occupying the coasts and islands from Kintyre north-

wards; the Picts, a native people whose speech may
have resembled that of the Britons but whose origins
are not completely clear, occupying the interior and
eastern coasts north of the Firth of Forth; the Britons,
speaking a form of early Welsh, occupying the central
valley and southern Scotland; and the Angles of the
English kingdom of Northumbria extending south-
wards from the Lothians. Amongst the Scots we know
that social organisation was strongly kinship based – a
characteristic not altogether dead today. Succession
lay not through the direct line but to the male best
fitted to inherit, the *tanaisdear*. Defence – and in the
earliest days occupancy of territory were undertaken
by *fianna*, armed warrior bands led by an heroic chief.
From these earliest days, surviving chronicles in
Gaelic ('Old Irish' but equally shared by Scotland),
saga literature, and some surviving orally transmitted
Ossianic ballads tell us much concerning the organisation of the people, their customs and values.

The Church was organised into family-like communities of priest-monks. Their abbots or leaders
might be termed bishops but they had no diocese in
the modern sense. They might take the whole of the
known or reachable world for their parish. Gaelic-
speaking missionaries and monks travelled the North
Atlantic, Britain and Europe as far as Italy and Kiev.
These were the people making up the vital link as
culture-bearers who restored civilisation to Europe.
Their cultural influence can be seen in the northern
English kingdoms; a Northumbrian king Aldfrid (d.
708) was one of the leading Gaelic poets of the 7th
century, *Fland Fína mac Ossu*. These cultural influences can further be traced to Alcuin and the culture
he brought with him from northern England to the

Court of Charlemagne and to the refugee monks fleeing from the Sack of Iona by the Vikings, welcomed at his court. Before the reversal of influence of the Gaelic church at the Synod of Whitby, Gaelic had become a principal *lingua franca* of northern Britain.

The Scots absorbed their neighbours, the Picts, possibly by a union of crowns through a common heir. The Gaelic-speaking state extended across the whole of Scotland north of the Clyde-Forth line; after 844 A.D. the succession of Kenneth Mac Alpin produced the first king of the Picts and Scots. Gaelic seems to have supplanted fairly rapidly whatever language the Picts spoke in this early period, for the combined military and political strength of the Picts and Scots spread Gaelic speech into the Welsh-speaking area of southwestern Scotland (Strathclyde) in the following centuries and also into the Anglian region of the Lothians. Following the Battle of Carham (1018) the Gaelic Scots had achieved pre-eminence throughout the area we know today as Scotland and – for a time – beyond, into Cumbria and Northumberland. The occurrence of Gaelic speech in these areas is witnessed by surviving placenames. Up until this stage, the only reversion to the Gaelic speech community was in the Northwest, where Viking settlements established Norse speech in the Northern Isles, Hebrides and Northwest seaboard. With the exception of Shetland, Orkney and Caithness where Norn survived into the modern period, a mixed Norse-Gaelic community came into being: the 'Gall-Gael'. Gaelic dress (adopted for example by Magnus Barelegs) and Gaelic names and naming customs were readily taken over and the incomers were after a while effectively Gaelicised. It is in fact the descen-

dants of these people who are the present-day surviving Gaelic speech-community.

Gaelic influences in the Church survived the Synod
of Whitby and the eventual recognition of the religious supremacy of Rome in Scotland. The secular
bardic orders and schools were organised in three
grades: *Ollamh* (doctor), *fili,* (master), and *bard* (bachelor) and the three ranks within the Columban
church were similar in appearance: *seniores, operarii
fratres* and *alumni.* Great store was set on learning and
appointments within the church lay in the gift of the
ferleighinn (man of learning) – an office which survived in Scotland into the 13th century.

By the 11th century, therefore, Gaelic clearly came
to be the language of social dominance throughout
Northern Britain – perhaps dominating generally
north of the Tweed, with a cultural influence extending at least to the Tyne. It was the language of an
impressive culture which had influenced Anglo-
Saxon England and beyond – had indeed brought
literacy to the English, and brought civilisation back
to Europe. Gaelic was the language of the Scottish
state, its royal house, the language of learning and the
church. Through Gaelic the arts of writing, scholarship and classical civilisation had been returned to
much of Britain and the continent. In the Scottish
society of the 11th century, Gaelic was the medium
through which government and administration were
carried on. An integrated Gaelic society had come
into existence in Northern Britain, deciding its own
affairs, influencing the course of world events.

For what reasons therefore did the displacement of
Gaelic come about? Why did Gaelic fail to maintain
itself as the national speech of the Scots? For from the

mid-11th century Gaelic was already in the process of being shifted out of these positions. We take it so much for granted that today the Scots are an English-speaking people that references – say, in Bede – to the speech of the Scots fails to register upon the general reader that this was other than the Scottish English of today or an earlier variant of it. A dramatisation of the life of St Margaret on schools radio some years ago for instance, failed to convey the fact that St Margaret came to a land and a court in which English was a completely foreign and alien language, known only to those few who had travelled or had relations with the English kingdoms far to the south. Yet, unless such facts are effectively conveyed, how can we give faithful impressions of our origins and life and relationships in earlier times?

It is undoubtedly misleading to read back into the circumstances of the 11th century such modern concepts such as national and official languages. But Gaelic at that time predominated throughout most of what we now call Scotland and was the language of its rulers. We do not know to what extent Gaelic was widely spoken throughout southern Scotland. Gaelic certainly established itself in Ayrshire and Galloway. In the southwest the Britons had spoken a similar Celtic language and placenames show that hybridisation of Gaelic and early Welsh occurred. 'British' speech seems to have survived, though, at least until the reign of David I (1124-1153) in Strathclyde. Elsewhere in the southwest a shift from British to Gaelic forms of speech was probably general. In the Lothians Gaelic was initially a superimposed form of speech: the language of the governing class and the everyday speech of particular villages and centres –

perhaps those which have retained their Gaelic names to the present day. However, surviving documents show that Gaelic was in use amongst ordinary people well into the middle ages – serfs, for example, having typically Gaelic names.

At this point Scotland, the land of the Scots (those who spoke Gaelic) had come into being, governed by a Gaelic-speaking monarchy ruling through a Gaelic-speaking court and extending its influence through-out a predominantly Gaelic- speaking nation by means of seven provincial rulers, the *Mormaers* (great stewards) heads of great Gaelic houses and through them to the *toiseachs* (thanes) of each local district. What is now to be accounted for is the shift to English, the speech of its southern neighbour and traditional enemy in the medieval period, by a people who remained politically and militarily independent. Why and how did the Scots trade in the language of saints and scholars for English as the language of the Scottish State?

THE RISE OF SCOTTISH NATIONHOOD

Gaelic was closely bound up with the formation of Scottish nationhood. This should not be a surprisingly outrageous idea. But if it is so, it is because we have lost sight of the fact that Gaelic was the principal language of civilisation, culture and government in early medieval Scotland. If today Gaelic is on the fringes of national life, this fact should not blind us to the reality that in the national life of Scotland in the early middle ages, Gaelic stood at the centre.

As has been noted, the shift of Gaelic from this central position began from the mid-11th century onwards; but the process was gradual and the account of this shift spreads over several centuries. Probably to the people of the times no appreciable change was occurring; yet inexorable changes there were and, as the centuries passed, these changes gathered momentum.

Although Gaelic began to be displaced first in central and southern Scotland, writers as late as the 16th. century show us how slow and how partial this process had been. John Major, writing in 1521, states that 'most of us spoke Irish a short time ago' and that by his day 'one half of Scotland speaks Irish'. Hector Boece (circa 1527) dates the coming of English to Norman influences and the subsequent settlement of Englishmen and to *'jeopardeis and chance of battall'*, for *'those of us who live on the borders of England have forsaken our mother tongue and learned English, being driven thereto by wars and commerce but the Highlanders remain just as they were at the time of Malcolm Canmore in whose days we began to adopt English'*. Sir Thomas Craig, writing during the reign of James VI, recalled from personal memory substantial survival of Gaelic-speaking communities in Stirlingshire and Dunbartonshire. Other later commentators, for example Kennedy, in his *Flyting with Dunbar*, blame the heavy loss of life occasioned by the treachery of the Earl of March and Dunbar in the Wars of Independence.

There were at least five chief ways in which Gaelic Scotland was culturally penetrated by Anglo-Norman England after 1057. The first of these – and perhaps not the most important – was the court itself. When Malcolm Canmore *(Calum Ceann Mór* – Calum Big Head) came to the throne he had spent some years in refuge in England. He took as his bride, Margaret, the grand-daughter of Edmund Ironside of the Wessex and English royal house. Margaret had spent her earlier years in exile in Hungary before she and her brother, Edward Atheling, representative of the Saxon royal line, took refuge at the court of Malcolm III. Unlike most Scotsmen of the time, Calum was

unusual in that he 'knew the English language quite
as well as his own' and thus he was able to act as
interpreter between his queen and the Scottish bishops. St Margaret's influence in anglicising the Scottish royal house may have been overstressed. England
came under Norman-French influences after 1066
and William had little cause to refrain from making
war upon a power which had welcomed the represen-
tatives of the legitimate English royal house. What
Margaret did achieve was a heightened demand for
new lines of trade – luxury goods as we might today
say – chiefly taking the form of embellishments for
the churches. This stimulated trading relations with
England for goods not able to be supplied at home.
However, it is also clear that Scottish institutions were
increasingly feudalised from this time on and this
seems to have been associated with the settlement of
Anglo-Normans who were granted lands by the
crown. Here again, we must remember these incomers were French – not English-speaking – and Isobel
Grant, and later authorities such as John Bannerman,
drew attention to the mass of evidence indicating
substantial survival of Gaelic in personal names in the
documents of central and southern Scotland
throughout the middle ages.

There was a substantial survival too of Gaelic public officials (for example the *brehon*: the *britheamh* or
judge; the *toiseach:* the thane or steward; the *ferleighinn* or man of learning) as well as Gaelic forms of
taxation and land measurement within feudal lowland society. Medieval life in Scotland, whether 'highland' or 'lowland', was underlain by the retention and
adaption of Gaelic institutions. Scotland adopted aspects of feudalism that were felt autonomously

necessary, unlike England where an alien feudal system was imposed by conquest. For example, there was no manorial system in Scottish feudalism.

Secondly, then, feudalisation in Scotland imported new social concepts, new terms, new forms of social organisation and the influx of new people, often resulting in co-existence of new and old ways for considerable periods of time. Feudalism linked with Norman penetration of Scottish society, got well under way by the reign of David I (1124-1153). As Norman-French speech gave way to English among the landed classes in England, so it may be imagined a similar shift occurred amongst their kinsfolk in Scotland. That French gained ascendancy in the Scottish court is clear. There was no direct shift from Gaelic to English.

English itself came into Scotland by way of very different classes of people: originally through the Angles of Northumbria who had annexed and settled Lothian, and in the middle ages by merchants and tradesfolk from England and the Low Countries. Burghs began to be established in the 11th and 12th centuries. These were really trading posts and market stances. William of Newburgh, writing in 1174, described how they were established and run by foreigners of whom the Flemings were the most important. These merchants from the Low Countries spoke a Germanic dialect not very different from the English of those days. Through the establishment of burghs in central and eastern Scotland, much of Scotland's overseas trade came to be in the hands of Flemish and English-speakers.

The Scottish capital or seat of the royal court had traditionally been located in the Gaelic heartland of

Perth and Fife. (For example at Dunkeld, Scone, Perth or Dunfermline.) With the passage of time, the royal House of Canmore relocated the court within the partially Anglian Lothians, thus strengthening the anglicising trends in the speech of the Scottish court when they came.

Lastly, as the result of war, the occupation of parts of southern Scotland by English forces provided further language contacts in favour of English. There were English refugees who settled in Scotland after William harried Northern England. It is probable also that casualties among the Gaelic-speaking forces of the Scottish state reduced the Gaelic-speaking population of southern Scotland, removing many of its leaders and perhaps leaving the surviving women-folk to marry amongst the incomers.

The operation of these five factors together first brought about a shift from Gaelic to French in the court, the royal family and some of the principal nobility. Next, a shift to English speech seems to have extended from the Lothians into the Western Low-lands and outward from the burghs along the coastal plain of the northeast, assisted by the 'plantation' of the Gaelic province of Moray. The evolution of Low-land Scots from the Anglian speech of the Lowlands started to take place but as the community language shifted from Gaelic to English, Gaelic influences re-mained embedded in popular speech giving to Lal-lans its distinctively Scottish characteristics. In like manner, the customs and folk beliefs of the lowland people remained strongly Gaelic.

Gaelic was superseded as the everyday speech in Central Scotland between 1157 and 1400. Exactly when is difficult to say, because written documents survive in Latin, French, and then English. As English began to be used for official documents in the 12th century the evidence for survival of Gaelic amongst the Lowlanders lies in the use of Gaelic personal names which these documents record. In the Northeast Lowlands Gaelic certainly remained the everyday speech and the 'official' language as the Book of Deer records land grants during this period in Gaelic. Barrow (in Gillies, 1989) has recently shown how tenuous Gaelic was during the middle ages in this part of Scotland. Gaelic was evidently displaced fairly rapidly in the south and later in the east. In the southwest the survival of Gaelic into the 18th century is a matter of historical fact. Here, in Galloway and Carrick, the language certainly survived as a vernacular in general use into the 16th century and in more isolated pockets throughout the 17th century. It has been claimed also that Gaelic communities survived in Fife up to this time.

As Gaelic speech and its associated customs and way of life were displaced in southern Scotland there were some spirited rearguard actions. We cannot project our present-day ideas backwards into the past and say that these were Gaelic revolts aimed at re-establishing Gaelic at the centre of national life or promoting a Gaelic revival as such. However, there were substantial revolts against an Anglo-Norman establishment conducted by Gaelic-speaking leaders and mobilising Gaelic-speaking areas of the country. No doubt they did desire to re-establish the supremacy of their own people and their own way of life. Their struggle was not simply one to conserve an older way of life. For example, Fergus, the Prince, Lord or ruler of Galloway, a leader of two Gaelic rebellions, was widely travelled in England, Wales and Ireland and introduced innovations into the church organisation of the southwest in the times of David I.

With Gaelic support Donald Bane (Domhnall Bàn – Donald the Fair) seized the crown from his brother Malcolm II in 1093. Twice in the reign of David I (1124-53), Fergus of Galloway revolted against Norman influences in court and state. During the same reign a revolt of the Gaelic province of Moray was also put down (1130). Moray again revolted in 1187. At the Battle of the Standard (1138), a motley army containing each of the chief ethnic groups under the rule of David I King of Scots faced the forces of the northern English barons. The army comprised, according to Richard of Hexham: 'Normans, Germans, English, Northumbrians, Cumbrians, men of Teviotdale and Lothian, Picts who are commonly called Galwegians, and Scots'. The most Gaelic of the native nobility Malise *(Maol-Iosa)* of Strathearn championed the rights of the Gaelic Scots to lead the battle and so each ethnic group fought in separate order – with disastrous results. In the ensuing rout of the 'Scottish' army, the Scots – the Gaelic speakers – turned alike upon the other ethnic groups fleeing with them. By 1234 the Gaelic principality of Galloway was finished. The death of Aidan, the last lord, without male heir resulted in a final rebellion which was subdued by Alexander II.

This was far from being the end of Gaelic power in Scotland. With the steady decline in power of Norway, the mixed Gaelic- Norse people of the Hebrides and Northwest asserted themselves and established a principality which was effectively independent of the

King of Scots throughout the rest of the middle ages. The Lordship of the Isles had its origin in the Viking kingdom of Sodor and Man. About the middle of the 12th century a leader emerged in this area called Somerled *(Somhairle)* who seized much of the Scottish possessions of the last Norse King of Man, and established himself by force-of-arms as 'Regulus and Thane of Argyll', having achieved supremacy throughout the Western Isles and coastlands from Kintyre and Bute northwards. Until the forfeiture of the Lordship of the Isles in 1493 and the subsequent failure of Clan Donald and its allies permanently to revive its powers and rights in the 16th century there thus remained within Scotland a centre of Gaelic power and an integrated Gaelic society, acknowledged even by Lowland writers to have best preserved the manners, speech and customs of the Scots. Bishop Leslie said, writing in 1578, that the Highlanders to *'this day speik the ald scottis toung, planelie have the selfe sam maneris ... that nocht oulie ... they have keipet the toung hail uncorupte; bot lykewyse the maner of cleithing and leiving'.*

During the middle ages, Gaelic did not cease abruptly to have any connection with the Scottish monarch and state. Most of the mainland area of Scotland remained Gaelic-speaking and although by the time of Bannockburn, Fordoun, (writing between 1363 and 1383) might state: 'The Highlanders and people of the Islands are a savage and untamed nation ... hostile to the Anglic people and language', we must remember that at this time many 'Lowland' people were still Gaelic-speaking. Moreover, however hostile the Highlanders and Islanders might have been towards Scotland's 'Anglic' peoples, the

Lordship of the Isles entered into treaty relationships with the English crown, as witnessed by the later Treaty of Westminster-Ardtornish of 1462, in which a partition of the Scottish kingdom was agreed. As late as the reign of Alexander III, surviving manuscripts record and depict the traditional recitation of the royal pedigree by a Gaelic seanchaidh or professional historian on the occasion of the King's accession in 1249. The death of Alexander III in 1285/6 brings to an end the House of Canmore under which Gaelic customs − for example the accession ceremonies − had been perpetuated and amongst whom some official usage of Gaelic had been retained.

Yet essentially by this time the Kings of the Scots had become in language, culture and sympathy completely French. Walter of Coventry wrote in 1212: 'For the more recent kings of Scots profess themselves to be rather Frenchmen, both in race and manners, language and culture; and after reducing the Scots to utter servitude, they admit only Frenchmen to their friendship and service.'

With the royal and noble governing class French in speech, the rising burghal merchant class was preponderantly English. By the 13th century Gaelic had ceased to be a socially dominant language. Except in the Highlands and Hebrides, where it conserved and developed an integrated culture, Gaelic in central and southern Scotland was restricted to the common people although territorially the greater part of Scotland whether 'Highland' or 'Lowland' was Gaelic-speaking. The core society of early medieval Scotland was in fact trilingual; a situation rather like that in Java, Siam and Indo-China, where there are three languages in use in different levels of society: royal, honorific and common. Or, like a trilingual society in Southern India, a symbiotic relationship of three occupational castes, speaking different languages. This interesting socio-linguistic situation has been stable for some time in India, Java and South-east Asia but it was superseded fairly rapidly in central Scotland at least, where English made headway in the manner already described.

However Gaelic was not altogether ignored by the royal houses which succeeded the House of Canmore. Robert Bruce having achieved the throne with 'Highland' assistance, inflicted one of the most decisive defeats an English army has ever received at Bannockburn, carrying as standard into the battle the Brecbennoch of St Columba, the most sacred relic of Gaelic Scotland. He then turned his attention to securing his own kingdom and extending his influence in Ireland. He called a Parliament at Ardchattan in Argyll and naturally enough its proceedings were in Gaelic. In Ireland Bruce urged the Irish to common cause with the Scots for, he said, that the two peoples shared a common origin, common customs and common language.

Scotland's last Gaelic-speaking monarch was James IV (1488- 1513) who cultivated Highland music and employed many highland servants and harpers. He travelled in the Highlands and had taken the trouble to learn the language of his northern subjects. (It is interesting that at the present time it is felt desirable that the heir to the throne, as Prince of Wales, should in like manner learn Welsh – a promise originally made by Edward I but never kept. With the forfeiture of the Lordship of the Isles and the assumption of the

title by the heir to the throne perhaps, the acquisition
of the language of his future Highland subjects by the
crown prince might restore fairplay all round.)

Within the Lordship of the Isles and within the
great Gaelic houses of the Highlands an integrated
Gaelic way of life continued throughout the middle
ages. It is true that a common language and a common culture continued to be shared by Gaelic Scotland and Gaelic Ireland, and there was little to
prevent the free coming and going of people across
the narrow seas which joined rather than separated
the Gaelic Lordship of the Isles with the then most
Gaelic of all the five provinces of Ireland, Ulster.
There were native learned orders of bardic poets,
seanchaidhs or historians, clerics and ecclesiastics,
latimers, judges, harpists and other musicians, harpists, scribes, physicians and the like. Their reputation
might be as great in Ireland as it was in Scotland and
they might have been almost as well travelled in the
one country as the other. In one famous instance as
Derick Thomson has shown, the MacMhuirich bardic
family, records of a continuous tradition exist from
the 13th century to circa 1800 – and longer if its
Canadian branch is taken into account. There was in
fact the one culture province of Gaeldom extending
from Cork and Kerry to Cape Wrath and the Hebrides. Considerable divergence between local dialects in Ireland and Scotland had commenced quite
early but until the 16th century the literary language
of the high culture remained unified. Although many
scholars refer to Old and Middle Irish, it would be
more in keeping with the actual circumstances of the
situation to call it Common Gaelic, following the modern Celtic scholar Kenneth Jackson.

Throughout Gaeldom there existed a common literary standard, mutually intelligible common speech, common oral traditions, dress, customs and life-style. Perhaps too much has been made of clan warfare, ignoring much of the internal strife which went on in England during the middle ages and later. Much of it was at the level of cattle raiding, a practice later celebrated in the 'wild west'. But despite such internal conflicts, integrative factors held Gaeldom together by a common culture and system of values. A chief might take his clan 'out' against a neighbour but the members of literary and learned orders could travel throughout Gaeldom unmolested and expect hospitality and a welcome at every great house they reached. Gaelic was the language of all levels of society. As a surviving land grant charter of the Lords of the Isles shows it was used alike for legal and official purposes. As an integral society Gaeldom was generally self-sufficient and, although its sphere of influence contracted towards the end of this period, it generally settled its own affairs and developed its own institutions in its own way – notably in the clan system: a novel and distinctive alternative to or variant upon the feudal system.

This independence was to be increasingly threatened by the growing power of the Scottish monarchy and state – especially after the Reformation. Nevertheless, before the loss of its effective independence Gaeldom demonstrated its capacity to innovate and to produce new culture. The clan system developed well beyond its parallels in Irish society. The hierarchical society of Gaelic Scotland was underpinned strongly by social bonds based upon kinship. The partriarchal chief was acknowledged as the blood relation to closer or lesser degree of his dependent chieftains, tacksmen and clansfolk. Yet the principle of tanistry provided for the selection of a cousin or brother who might be the better fitted to succeed. Traditional justice was vested in the chiefs until 1747.

New literary and musical models and forms developed within the high culture – for example the art-form of piobaireachd developed at the end of this period and such was the level of its cultivation by the school or order maintained by the MacCrimmon family under the patronage of the MacLeods that the pipes rapidly superseded the harp as the pre-eminent musical instrument of Gaelic Scotland. The classical symphonic music of the piobaireachd became above all other forms the distinctive pinnacle of Gaelic musical culture.

Until the assertion of royal power following the Scottish Reformation, Gaelic speech within the Gaelic area was a sufficient medium for all social uses. That it could be acceptable indeed as a language of learned cultivation outside its own boundaries we can see from the rules of Aberdeen Grammar School in 1553. The scholars might converse in Latin, Greek, Hebrew or Gaelic but not in English. In the ensuing decades such attitudes towards Gaelic within the Lowlands were radically to change, and as the result of the subsequent penetration of Gaelic Scotland by Lowland influences, the function of Gaelic within the remaining Gaelic-speaking area was itself to change. Throughout almost all the Lowlands by the end of the middle ages English had become the common speech of all classes and no longer just the language of dominant social and occupational groups. From about 1520 onwards the common Lowland speech

came to be called 'Scots' and Gaelic identified as
'Irish'. Thus the Gaelic language and its speakers
came to be regarded as in some way alien within their
own nation. The traditional society of Gaelic Scotland
was to be drawn into the same political and cultural
sphere as Lowland Scotland after the Reformation
had removed the one common cultural and symbolic
institution shared by both: the Roman Catholic
Church.

"MÌ-RÙN MÓR NAN GALL"

'Mhair i fòs
Is cha téid a glòir air chall
Dh'aindeoin gò
Is mi-rùn mhóir nan Gall.'
Alasdair mac Mhaighstir Alasdair:
AISÉIRIGH NA SEANN CHANAIN GAIDHLIG

'It continues yet
And its glory shall not be lost
Despite the vilification
And great ill-will of the Lowlanders.'
Alasdair MacDonald:
'RESURRECTION OF THE ANCIENT
GAELIC LANGUAGE'

In these words, the 18th century bard Alasdair Mac-
Donald, celebrated the ancient Gaelic language. The
poet outlines the ways in which in history Gaelic had

been used in court and Parliament, by great and small, by Highlander and Lowlander. With the Lowlanders' loss of Gaelic, it became very clear to the Highlanders after 1560 just how great an ill-will could be generated against them. Indeed, a leading figure in the development of an 'anti-Gaelic ideology' was no less a figure than the King himself.

With the establishment of the Reformation, a number of shifts in relationship between Lowland and Highland Scotland came about. Since Highland areas despite Protestant inroads remained very largely Catholic after 1560, the language and life-style of Gaelic society were redefined as alien in references after this date. Gaelic, for example, ceases to be regarded or termed Scottish and is called Irish, Erse and the like, although it was in fact at this time that Gaelic was developing its distinctively Scottish forms characteristic of the Modern period. The terms 'Scottish' and 'Scots' came to be applied instead to Lowland speech and traditions. The Gaelic-speaking Scots of the Highlands and Islands could then be described as Irish and foreign or even as savage or barbarous. The writings of James VI show clearly the reformation of attitudes and the birth of a new ideology regarding Gaelic.

The equation was made of Gaelic with both barbarity and with 'popery'. The neutral tone of earlier documents relating to Gaelic had changed and was replaced by what amounted to 150 years of 'cold war' on the part of Lowland society against Gaelic society. Moreover, the categorisations of 'Highlander' and 'Lowlander' and inimical attitudes towards Gaelic and Gaelic culture are still present in Scottish popular opinion – and have even been accepted by the Highlanders themselves.

Scotland was one of the first European nations to pass legislation concerned with public education and the creation of a state educational system. The earliest Scottish education acts date back to 1494/96 and enjoined upon all lairds and chiefs the obligation of sending their children to learn Latin, 'art' and law in schools in the 'lowlands'. This meant that the formative years of the children of the leading citizens of Gaeldom were to be spent in an alien environment – a feature of Highland education which recurs throughout the educational history of Gaelic Scotland and remains alive to our own day.

In the post-reformation period, Gaelic was not perceived as constituting a language in its own right. The intention of the reformers was to put the vernacular scriptures into the hands of a literate nation, but Gaelic did not appear to them to be the means of accomplishing this. It seemed obvious to the reformers that a simultaneous shift could be made from Gaelic to English, from Catholicism to Calvinism, from barbarity to civility. Similar perceptions have been seen until recently in Australia where native languages were accorded no place in the educational schemes for aboriginal children. 'The native language is doomed anyway, why use it in education?' Other parallels exist with regard to Indian education in the U.S.A. Educational programmes have been criticised for failing to recognise and use the heritage of native lore and know-how which Indian children had brought with them to school. White teachers failed to perceive Indian culture as 'knowledge' and regarded the children as culturally 'empty', and their homeland as a 'wilderness'.

The Scottish Reformation brought into being changes in attitudes and relationships between Highland and Lowland Scotland. Politically the Reformation was accomplished by the supremacy of the pro-English party over the pro-French party and was ratified by the Treaty of Edinburgh 1560, Acts of the Scots Parliament in the same year and the drawing up of the 'First Book of Discipline' (1561) which outlined a constitution for the reformed church. This statement went much farther than ecclesiastical organisation for it contained an outline for a state education system encompassing parish elementary schools, town grammar schools and colleges, as well as bursaries to universities. A system of inspection at every level was added, and the finance was envisaged as forthcoming from sequestered church lands. The principles were further made explicit in the Assembly Act of 1562.

This was the intention of the reformers. It fell far short of realisation. So far as the universal provision of elementary schools was concerned, this ideal was not achieved until the nineteenth century. It was important for lowland society that schools should be provided throughout Scotland and notably in the Highland area. The inclusion of all ranks of society and the whole of the geographical area of Scotland into a unitary nation of common speech and values was important for the perpetuation of the new faith and order. The Act of 1494/6 was, however, a dead letter whether in Lowland or Highland Scotland. The Act of 1543 was, however, of more significance for the relations of Gaelic and Lowland Scotland. The Act gave authority for all citizens to possess the Scriptures 'baith in the new testament and the auld in the

Vulgar Toung Englis or Scottis'. This would seem to signify that in the then Catholic and non-Reformed Scottish State some measure of popular literacy existed – at least in English in Lowland Scotland – and that the admission of Gaelic as a national language enjoying any measure of recognition or equal validity with English Lowland speech was unrecognised or unrealised by Scotland's government.

The earliest education acts of the reformed Scots Parliament have a neutral attitude to Gaelic. The Act of 1567 ordained that all schools in town and country-side, all colleges and universities should be reformed (in religion) and likewise their masters. The Assembly Act of 1579 forebade studies abroad in Catholic countries and the Education Act of 1579 attempted to preserve 'song schools'. The 1582 Education Act ratified in similar terms its predecessor of 1567. That the presence of a non-reformed Catholic society of alien speech was seen as a menace to Lowland society and the Scottish state is clear from the terms and tones of the Education Acts of Scotland from the outset of the 17th century. However, in the latter part of the 16th century the attempts to destroy the integrity and autonomy of Gaelic society in Scotland were political, economic and military. In his *Basilikon Doron* of 1598(?) James VI observed of his Gaelic subjects: *'I shortly comprehend them all in two sorts of people: the one that dwelleth in our mainland that are barbarous for the most part, and yet mixed with some show of civility; the other that dwelleth in the Isles, and are utterly barbarians, without any sort of show of civility'.* The King's intention was to plant colonies among them of *'answerable inland subjects'* to *'reform and civilise'* them whilst *'rooting out and transporting the barbarous and stubborn sort'.* An Act of

1583 (The 'General Band') enjoined on the Highland chiefs the duty of giving sureties (i.e. hostages of their own kin) through landed men in the Lowlands for their good conduct. Further Acts of 1597 laid on the Highland chiefs a yearly rent to the Crown and the requirement of producing written title to their lands whilst a further act authorised the establishment of new burghs in the Highlands: in Kintyre, Lochaber and the Isle of Lewis.

The failure to establish burgh towns in the two latter districts may be linked with the failure of the 'Fife Adventurers' licensed by the Crown to settle and develop the Island of Lewis (1599-1610). It was intended that Harris, Northern Skye and Glenelg (which together with Lewis were forfeited MacLeod lands) were to have been settled also. The 1590s marked a period of repeated legislation and concern of the Privy Council for law and order in the Highlands and Islands. Incursions into the area to enforce the laws, collect rents and punish defection became increasingly severe and effective. The legitimisation of these activities was seen (at least by the king) in terms of *'planting the Gospell'* and *'Godis feare'* among the *'wild savages'* but also with the rider of *'ressaving the dew rentis addebtit to us'*. Shortly the continuing unreformed character of the Highlanders was to be identified as much with their Gaelic language as with their Catholic religion.

In Ireland and Scotland initially successful Gaelic revolts in 1595 led to renewed armed activities aimed at supplanting Gaelic power. In Ireland the Flight of the Earls, the collapse of Gaelic society, especially in Ulster, the most Gaelic of the provinces, and its subsequent plantation by Lowland Scots and English

protestant settlers effectively destroyed the contacts
between Irish and Scottish Gaeldom. After the collapse of O'Dogherty's rebellion in 1608, Chichester,
the leader of the King's forces in Ireland having
enjoyed some measure of support from fencible
troops from south-west Scotland offered his aid for a
projected Scottish venture into the Western Isles on
the grounds that these tasks 'were but two parts of
one and the same work'. James, the first King of
Scotland, England and Ireland, looked for the settlement of the borderlands between his three realms
such that they might become the peaceful midland
shires of one kingdom.

In 1609 were drawn up the 'Statutes of Iona'.
Twelve Highland and Hebridean chiefs were enticed
aboard a ship expecting to hear a sermon. The armed
expedition to the Isles under Andrew, Lord Stewart
of Ochiltree, and Andrew Knox, Bishop of the Isles,
secured a written bond of these chiefs after they had
undergone a period of imprisonment in the Lowlands. The agreement thus entered into under duress
provided for the provision and support of protestant
ministers to Highland parishes, the establishment of
hostelries, the outlawing of beggars, the prohibition
of traditional hospitality and strong drink, the education of chiefs' heirs in Lowland schools where they
'may be found able sufficiently to speik, reid and wryte
Englische', limitation on the bearing and use of arms,
the outlawry of bards and other bearers of the traditional culture and a prohibition on the protection of
fugitives.

This enaction was the first of a succession of
measures taken by the Scottish government specifically directed towards the extirpation of the Gaelic

language, the destruction of its traditional culture and the suppression of its bearers. Traditional forms of Gaelic learning were not recognised as knowledge by the authorities. Literacy in Gaelic did not count as literacy in the eyes of official policy. The language itself came to lack official status as civilised speech. (Such views were to persist even up to the present day in attitudes which admit or provide little place in the curriculum of Scottish or Highland schools for the teaching of the language or instruction in the history or culture of Gaelic Scotland.) The Statutes of Iona were ratified by an Act of the Privy Council of 1616 whose preface explicitly connects the lack of true religion, civility, godliness, knowledge and learning with the persistence of Gaelic speech and seeks to redress these deficiences with universal establishment of English as the common language and seeks to implement this by the establishment of schools:

'Forasmekle as the kingis Majestie haveing a speciall care and regaird that the trew religioun be advanceit and establisheit in all the pairtis of this kingdome, and that all his Majesties subjectis, especiallie the youth, be exercised and trayned up in civilitie, godliness, knowledge and learning, that the vulgar Inglishe toung be universallie plantit, and the Irishe language, which is one of the cheif and principall causis of the continewance of barbaritie and incivilitie amongis the inhabitantis of the Iles and Heylandis, may be abolisheit and removit; and quhairas thair is no means more powefull to further this his Majesties princelie regaird and porpois than the establisheing of schooles in the particular parrocheis of this kingdome whair the youthe may be taught at the least to write and reid, and be catechiesed and instructed in the groundis of religioun; thairfore the kingis Majestie, has thocht it necessary and expedient that in everie

parroche of this kingdome where convenient meanes may be had for interteyning a schoole, that a schoole sall be establisheit, and a fitt persone appointit to teache the same ...'

In these terms the Statutes of Iona were prefaced, legitimated and ratified by the Scottish Privy Council in its Education Act of 1616.

These measures may be viewed as an attempt to destroy the social customs of hospitality in the great houses of the Gaelic chiefs. The payments for the sustentation of travelling bards, musicians, historians and the other learned persons were made illegal. Such people, as well as many of the king's Gaelic-speaking subjects, might be regarded as either vagabonds or bards – in either case a category under prohibition – and thus summarily condemned to imprisonment, the stocks or transportation. Thus the Gaelic learned orders and the native high culture might be suppressed. As the links with Ireland were broken, Gaelic Scotland was thrown upon its own resources and then drawn into the cultural system of Lowland Scotland. The Highlands and Islands were thus rendered a cultural as well as a political dependency of Central (Lowland) Scotland. The establishment of the English language through the medium of a school system was seen as a principal means of achieving this social re-orientation. Such a policy was a recurrent theme of Scottish legislation in a series of education acts of the Scots Parliament and resolution of the General Assembly of the Church of Scotland for the next 150 years.

These resolutions were not implemented on any particularly general scale and the success of this policy was limited. No general parish school system was in practice achieved within the Highland area neither was any general literacy or common use of English established within this period. In fact, between the Commonwealth period and the accession of William and Mary, Gaelic society enjoyed some respite and the anti-Gaelic education acts were for this time repealed and suspended. However, the effective social separation of Scottish from Irish Gaeldom and the enforcement of the Statutes of Iona broke down the Gaelic learned orders and initiated the anglicisation of the chiefs. With the replacement of traditional economic links of the Highland area overseas by links through the Lowlands, Gaelic Scotland was effectively being drawn into the political system of the Scottish State.

At this point in the linguistic history of Scotland an interesting social process is at work: the legitimisation of the suppression of the original speech and continuing original culture of the Scottish nation by a religious party which had come into political power. In the 16th century literary references to Gaelic readily acknowledge it to be the Scottish language and the speech of Lowland Scotland within recent historical times. The Anglian speech of the Lowlands was referred to as *'Inglis'* (English). The remoteness of the Highland area from the Central Lowlands and its separate culture rendered the spread of new ideas and new values such as Calvinism slow and uncertain. The neutral tone in earlier 16th century documents relating to Gaelic underwent a change. This would have been difficult to accomplish had Gaelic been equated (as until recently it had been) with Scottish in the popular mind. Gaelic thus ceased to have an obvious relationship with Scottish nationality. The resulting animosities can still be recognised at the present time and identified by Gaels as *'mi-rùn mór nan Gall'* (the great ill-will of the Lowlanders).

The failure of the efforts of the Lowlanders to achieve their ends by legislation, armed incursion and economic penetration of the Highlands during the 17th century resulted in some revision of attitudes to Gaelic. By the end of the century there was a willing-ness in official quarters to use the language as a missionising medium.

During the 17th century a series of enactions had attempted to eradicate Gaelic and replace it by Eng-lish. The Statutes of Iona were confirmed by the Scottish Parliament in 1631. In 1633 Parliament passed a *'Ratification of the Act of Counsall Anent Planta-tioun of Schooles'* to apparently little effect.

In 1646 the General Assembly of the Church of Scotland passed a resolution to enforce the Statutes of Iona and to set up English schools in each Highland parish. An Act to these effects was passed in Parlia-ment in the same year. In 1662 the Act was repealed by the Restoration Parliament but after the Revol-ution of 1688 rents from the bishoprics of Argyll and Dunkeld were utilised for the *'erecting of English Schools for rooting out the Irish language and other pious uses'*. Acts of 1690 and 1693 were intended to provide teachers of proved political and religious loyalty and in 1696 the matter of the Act of 1646 was yet again restored to the Statute Book as the 'Act of Settling Schools'.

This last Act, however, specifically placed upon Kirk sessions in the parishes the clear duty of organis-ation and provided the necessary financial arrange-ments and by 1698 for example, some 43 schools were established in Argyll and the Isles. After 1690 the General Assembly of the Church of Scotland became especially conscious of the need to provide Gaelic-speaking Presbyterian clergy in the Highlands, (by Acts of the Assembly of 1701, 1710, 1714 and 1717). Acts of the Assembly in 1699 '*Anent Planting of the Highlands*' go into great detail in ensuring a supply of Gaelic-speaking clergy and church officials and 'Irish' Bibles and catechisms. That some change in attitudes to Gaelic were occurring may be read into the clause authorising a revision of the Irish Bible into the 'Highland Language'. Yet the sole language of instruction in the Highland Schools was English and in general was to remain so throughout the coming century.

A century of legislation proved ineffectual in supplanting Gaelic in the Highlands. Yet during this period the social organisations of the Gaelic cultural system underwent profound changes. The economic bases of support for the bardic schools had been removed and this species of literary and musical institution collapsed. Musicians and poets continued to be retained as individual professionals in the retinues of chiefs but the 17th century is the last in which there are notices of Scottish musicians and literati visiting Ireland and vice-versa. The compositions and culture continued to be transmitted, notably through the family, but the learned orders had lost their status and prestige. The compositions and traditions of the high culture were passed on to tradition-bearers lower in the social scale and the medieval high culture of Gaelic Scotland became transmuted into a folk-art. In some respects this resulted in a freer and livelier literary form taken by popular poets such as Iain Lom, Alasdair mac Mhaighstir Alasdair, Iain MacCo-

drum, Donnchadh Bàn Mac-an-t-Saoir, Rob Donn
MacAoidh, Màiri nighean Alasdair Ruaidh in the
17th and 18th centuries. Thus a new form of literary
art displaced the old: the composition by popular
poets of sophisticated oral production, not in response to professional patronage or for payment but
for personal satisfaction and the entertainment of a
peasant-type community of which the poet was part
(whether lettered, learned or neither). Naturally
themes and verse forms showed development beyond
the stereotyped classic production of the bardic
schools.

THE BREAKING OF
GAELIC SOCIETY

During the 18th century a society entitled the Society
in Scotland for Propagating Christian Knowledge
(S.S.P.C.K.), founded in 1701, became the chief
agency for the establishment of schools in the Gaelic
area and the promotion of English. In practice 'Christian knowledge' was, in the curriculum, equated with
the English language, the Presbyterian religion,
church music and arithmetic, those being the sole
subjects of instruction. Finance was attracted from
private subscribers, the General Assembly of the
Church of Scotland, church collections in the Lowlands, the State and the King. Attendance was voluntary but coercion and economic enducements were
from time to time reported.

Notwithstanding the pains taken by the Church of
Scotland to ensure a supply of Gaelic-speaking ministers to Gaelic charges, it is remarkable to encounter
references to prohibitions on the use of Gaelic as a

medium of instruction in S.S.P.C.K. minutes. Despite
the provision of the catechism and Metrical Psalms in
Gaelic it is incongruous to encounter instances of
S.S.P.C.K. schoolmasters being reprimanded for
teaching children to read these books in their schools
and being forbidden to teach children to read the
Irish Bible (a Scottish Gaelic version was not then
available). Only the English Bible might be used together with other English devotional works taught
mechanically. Not surprisingly, literacy in English
made little headway. It is known, however, that
Catholic 'hedge-schools' existed during this period.
The activities of Irish and Scottish Gaelic Catholic
priests is attested during this period and it is surmised
that their medium of teaching was Gaelic. One can
hardly imagine their mission being conducted in
English – a language utterly unknown to their hearers
(yet this was in fact the situation in the S.S.P.C.K.
schools).

A change in attitude to Gaelic in this educational
work was not possible until after the collapse of political Jacobitism in 1746 and the assurance of success in
pacifying the Highlands in the ensuing two decades.
Dr Samuel Johnson was instrumental in bringing
before the general public the fact that the S.S.P.C.K.
was actively preventing a translation of the Bible into
Scottish Gaelic from being published. Johnson attacked the policy of the S.S.P.C.K. towards the Highlanders in these terms:

' ... there remains only their language and their
poverty. Their language is attacked on every side.
Schools are erected in which English only is taught
and there were lately some who thought it reasonable
to refuse them a version of the Holy Scriptures, that

they might have no monument of their mother tongue.'

Boswell stated that he believed this letter of 1766 to be the finest work from Johnson's pen.

It is difficult to understand why Johnson is popularly believed to have been anti-Scottish and anti-Gaelic. It is true he once declared, erroneously, that no book had ever been written in Gaelic; but he also championed the production of literature in Gaelic and advocated the establishment of a Gaelic press in Skye.

The Gaelic New Testament of the S.S.P.C.K. appeared the following year in 1767 and the Old Testament was to follow in 1801. The S.S.P.C.K. schools from 1767 admitted Gaelic as the medium of instruction in their Highland schools (although parish schools continued to use English only).

A confrontation of two disparate societies was now taking place: each had its own distinctive cultural patterns, social structures, religious institutions and life-style which can be illustrated in the 'culture-clash' of their two languages. Lowland Scotland made plain its anxiety concerning the unreformed society in the north in terms of unease concerning its language, which was identified as the chief cause of barbarity, ignorance and popery. Gaelic society was reluctant to become absorbed within a society whose speech and institutions were alien, notwithstanding the consciousness amongst Gaelic tradition-bearers that theirs was the original and continuing 'Scottish' language and culture and that the incorporation of the Highlands into the Scottish state was being undertaken in the name of loyalty and obedience to the Scottish crown.

It is thus not surprising that the Jacobite Revolts in 1715 and, more particularly, of 1745, were readily supported by the majority of the Gaelic chiefs and their clansmen. Even in the case of clans like the MacLeods whose chiefs did not respond, large numbers of their clansfolk did. Resentment over the growing cultural interpenetration of the Highlands by institutions mediated through English, sporadic coercion to support governmental requirements and the new English schools and similar social tensions could, after the Union of 1707 with England and the accession of a non-Scottish dynasty to the British throne in 1714, enable Gaeldom to voice its sense of oppression against an entirely non-Scottish partner in the Union which had achieved conspicuous dominance, and against a German monarch with the passing of the Stuarts.

Culture-conflict was apparent in the imposition on the Gaelic Highlands of English language schools and the interference by agencies of the State in the cultural system of Gaeldom (the suppression of bardic schools and the withholding of scriptures in Gaelic, for example). Conflict in the form of armed risings resulted. The failure of Gaelic Scotland to maintain its political and military autonomy led to the 'pacification' of the Highlands by the Duke of Cumberland and to the Disarming Acts. These removed from the Highlanders not only their traditional social leaders and their weapons, but also made illegal the visible aspects of their material culture: their Highland Dress and their musical instruments, the pipes. After 1746 the social structure of the clan system was broken and a landlord and tenant relationship substituted. The remaining integrative aspects of Gaelic culture were removed: dress, music and the means of defence, with the exception only of the language itself and the popular oral folk-poets. The Jacobite chiefs were executed, punished and their lands forfeited. The surviving chiefs were forced by economic means into the position of landlords having contractual relations with their tenantry in the place of clan chiefs having familial relationships with their extended kin.

Hence a society based upon family, kin, clan was reformulated into one based upon a money economy. This was of increasing significance in a modern unified state well advanced into an industrial society, in which the industrial and agrarian revolutions were well under way. The Highlands were opened up for commercial exploitation and the institution of a greater division of labour in society. After 1746, greater economic activity in such enterprises as commercial forestry, extensive sheep farming, charcoal burning, civil engineering, iron-smelting and kelp-burning intensified economic life and brought greater interpenetration of the area by English speakers. Henceforward more activities and social situations in the Highlands were to become communicated through the English language. Economic innovation seems always to have been associated with intrusive use of English speech in Scotland.

The alienation of the Gaels from their traditional social leaders was in course of being accomplished as a language gap was being opened up between them. The process of alienation of the Gaels from the core society of modern Scotland was well under way. The alienation of the Gaels from their traditional culture had been attempted and a folk culture had arisen to replace it.

By the last few decades of the 18th century, Gaelic Scotland had been incorporated politically and economically into the United Kingdom. Though complete assimilation of Gaeldom socially and culturally had not yet been entirely accomplished, the traditional social structure was in decay, and intrusion of new economic institutions threatened the cohesion of the symbolic and value systems of Gaelic society.

The processes were essentially one-way: linguistic influence proceeded from English to Gaelic. Modification of Gaelic by English gathered momentum. English-Gaelic expressions increased in Gaelic speech. Highlanders most closely in contact with anglicising influences had of necessity to learn the incoming language and their original speech became redundant in economic and social life. Absorption proceeded as the Gaels adopted new institutions (e.g. a money economy) which are brought with the new language. New life-styles and customs are adopted and with them the associated new English forms of speech.

NEW RÔLES,
NEW SETBACKS

This period – from the introduction of the Gaelic
scriptures in 1767 to the Education (Scotland) Act of
1972 – is marked by the use of Gaelic as a means of
acculturating the Highland people into the mainstream of British society. The S.S.P.C.K. brought out
its Gaelic New Testament in 1767 and admitted
Gaelic into its schools as a medium of education,
notably insofar as religious instruction was concerned. The appearance of the scriptures in a vernacular Scottish Gaelic translation for the first time
was the beginning of a religious literature in Gaelic. It
is notable that the agencies of publication (chiefly the
S.S.P.C.K.) saw fit to provide translations only of
orthodox works which had been proven sound over
the passage of time.

Hence this religious literature was made up of the
most conservative of Puritan and Calvinist homiletics

of the previous century. These 'new' religious writings for the literate Gaels provided them with a fundamentalist predestinarian theology which remains active in the north-west and the northern Hebrides to the present day. Such a philosophy could be called upon by ministers of the Church of Scotland to justify the economic and social adversities brought upon the Highland people during this period as the wrath of God for their sins.

The period was also one of great economic difficulty in the Highlands. The traditional economy had been based upon subsistence agriculture and the pasturing of cattle. Surplus cattle were driven to the Lowlands and exchanged for money. Sheep were also common and pastured in equal ratio to cattle. By the later 18th century a money economy was being introducted into the Highlands: rents were sought in cash rather than kind. Some emigration was under way and had gained momentum as the result of increases in rents and the depersonalisation of relationships between chief or landlord and clanfolk or tenants. The intermediary class of 'tacksmen' (*fir-tac*) were being rendered redundant and there are instances of migrations of tacksmen who, as community leaders, took with them their dependent subtenants to lands of opportunity overseas.

The crucial factor which upset the balance of the Highland economy both in social and economic terms was the introduction of 'improved' varieties of sheep. The initial introduction of 'great sheep' which was to replace the small native multi-horned sheep was first undertaken in 1762 by Sir John Lockhart-Ross of Balnagowan in Easter Ross. The black-faced Lintons were the precursors of the more familiar Cheviot breed which by 1790 had reached the far north and whose husbandry was actively promoted by Sir John Sinclair of Ulster in Caithness. From 1790 sheep farming gained such momentum in the Highlands that the landowners with the prospect of good profits were enthusiastic in clearing from their lands the native Highland people and their settlements to enable clear leases to be made available to Lowland graziers.

The notorious Highland Clearances were undertaken in the face of popular resistance, frequently when the male population had been recruited to serve abroad in the armed forces, and, not surprisingly, often with violence and force. Such incidents commenced in Strath Rusdale, Ross-shire in 1792 and continued into the 1850s. Summary evictions avoiding the worse excesses of public violence were to continue until the passing of the Crofters Acts in 1886 and 1892.

As the result of the Clearances, whole areas were cleared of human beings and their native breeds of cattle and sheep. Ratios of twenty sheep to one of cattle were to ruin the pastoral viability of the land and to reduce wide areas to bracken, deer and grouse moor by the 20th century. It was in effect a human and an ecological disaster. Throughout the interior of the Gaelic mainland of the Highlands the first half of the 19th century witnessed the forced migration of virtually its entire population. In terms of the Gaelic speech community this could be regarded as the removal of its heartland. Effectively this was to reorientate the linguistic geography of Scotland in reducing the Gaelic areas to the very fringes of northern and western coastal areas and to the Hebrides.

During this period, the official use of Gaelic may be regarded as a means of accustoming the Highland people to an English-oriented way of life and of gaining their acquiescence in the adversities which were overcoming them and their way of life.

As has been noted, the S.S.P.C.K. schools after 1767 used Gaelic as a medium of instruction. Similarly, the schools set up by the commission administering forfeited Highland estates after 1746 followed the pattern of the S.S.P.C.K. schools. By the beginning of the 19th century it has been estimated that of a Highland population of some 335,000 about 300,000 understood Gaelic only. In 1824 the S.S.P.C.K. proposed that Gaelic-speaking children in its schools were first to read Gaelic before commencing with English. In 1828 Gaelic text books were introduced with assistance from the General Assembly of the Church of Scotland.

The success in the promotion of schools within the Highland area during this period may be gauged by the fact that in 1811 the S.S.P.C.K. maintained 290 schools educating 16,000 children throughout the Highlands and Islands. These schools, however, had not achieved any conspicuous success in promoting any general literacy or knowledge of English.

By the first quarter of the 19th century, migration of Gaels to the cities had resulted in colonies of urban Gaels now well accustomed to an urban way of life conducted through the medium of English and with sufficient means to promote charitable efforts in their former homelands. In 1811 was founded the Edinburgh Society for the Support of Gaelic Schools, and in 1812 and 1818 similar societies in Glasgow and Inverness. The policy of these societies was to teach initially solely through the medium of Gaelic with the first emphasis laid upon ensuring literacy in the Gaelic scriptures. In the case of Glasgow and Inverness Society schools, reading and writing in English was subsequently introduced through the medium of Gaelic. The schools were often temporary and their school masters travelled from village to village. Typically they taught all ages in shifts on weekdays, evenings and Sundays. The schools earned the popular epithet *Sgoilean Chriosd* (Schools of Christ) and it is estimated that by 1861 the Edinburgh Society alone had taught 100,000 persons to read and distributed some 200,000 Gaelic Bibles. Similar methods were used by *Comunn nam Ban* (The Free Church Ladies' Highland Association) set up following the disruption of 1843 and the secession of the Free Church from the Church of Scotland.

Further measures of the spread of popular Gaelic education in this period may be judged in the Inverness Society's report in 1826 of its 1822 survey. Some 495 schools had been established by then in the Highland area: 171 by the parishes of the Church of Scotland; 134 by the S.S.P.C.K.; 77 by the Edinburgh Society; 48 by the Glasgow Society; and 65 by the Inverness Society. The popular nature of this provision may be further judged in their attendance by Protestants and Catholics. Schools for Gaelic-speaking children were provided in Edinburgh, Aberdeen, Dundee and other urban centres. Schools of the S.S.P.C.K. had been established in Glasgow, Aberdeen, Dundee, Inverness, Perth and even London and other English cities. The extent to which Gaelic may have been used in these schools is not clear.

The Gaelic Society of London, established in 1777

to secure the repeal of the Disarming Acts which forbade use of the Highland dress, tartan and bagpipes after 1746, was successful in its objectives by the repeal measures of 1782 and 1784 which restored to lawful use these elements of Gaelic material and symbolic culture. This, the earliest Gaelic Society to be established, has continued in existence to the present day; in its early period it was active in charitable support of the Gaelic schools and in the relief of destitution in the Highland area. Famine conditions resulting from crop failures in 1835/36 and 1846/47 facilitated the evacuation of the mainland area.

The Gaelic Society of London also provided a translation service for the Government, putting into Gaelic the text of proclamations, Acts of Parliament and other notices for distribution and display in the Highland area. Thus Gaelic was in use for official purposes during this period and enjoyed some measure of governmental recognition. The original members of the Gaelic Society of London were probably in trade or the professions. The 1770s were a decade of very substantial emigration from the Highlands and Hebrides.

In the church, a strong Gaelic Protestant tradition had been founded. Through the diffusion of the scriptures in Gaelic, the utilisation of the Metrical Psalms in Gaelic and the widespread appointment of college-educated Gaelic-speaking ministers to Highland charges, a high standard of Gaelic preaching was promoted. Gaelic congregations developed a distinctive style of psalmody in which the metrical Psalms came to be sung to long tunes given out by the precentor and antiphonally answered with extemporised decoration by the congregation. Each of these aspects of Protestant church tradition continues to have a place of special regard with Gaelic congregations to the present day and they have been identified as the means whereby Gaelic has continued to have significance as a social institution.

It is clear, though, that the established church, the presbyterian Church of Scotland, was in this period a particularly useful agency of political and social control to the government and the landowning classes. A fatalistic, predestinarian theology was preached from pulpits at the time of harassments and evictions. Acquiescence towards the will of God as identified with the clearance policy of the landlord was frequently enjoined and acceptance of punishment for sins and waywardness was propounded. For many social activities a testimony of good behaviour from the parish minister might be required.

Effective resistance to eviction might be controlled by the withholding of such a certificate, which, amongst other things, would prevent a ceremony of marriage taking place or a tenancy being granted. That there was some acceptance of this designation of wickedness on the part of the evicted Highland people can be seen for instance in the graffiti on the church windows at Croick where evicted people from Glencalvie, Ross-shire, sheltered in 1845. Such acceptances of fate and adversity are also apparent in the doctrines and religious thought of Gaelic communities up to the present time.

However, in 1843 occurred an event in Scotland's ecclesiastical history known as the Disruption. It was a secession away from the Church of Scotland on the part of many of its Highland congregations and min-

isters. Although explained and justified by the seces-
sionists in doctrinal and religious terms such
explanations were clearly underpinned by a profound unease with the use made by the authorities of
the established church to sanction the clearances
which by the 1840s had reached their climax. The
landowners were unfavourably disposed in many instances to this newly formed 'Free Church'. Often feus
were unobtainable for the land on which to erect a
church. Instances occur in which ships were used as
places of worship as a result. The Free Church, however, despite persecution, emerged as the popular
church of the Gaelic peasantry in the northwest. By
1851 it had established the remarkable total of 712
schools in Scotland as a whole. Its language was that
of its people. Its strength lay in the Gaelic areas and
these facts remain so to the present day. The Free
Church – and a further secession, the Free Presbyterian Church – are the principal churches of the remaining Gaelic-speaking areas of the northwest and
northern Hebrides.

In this period Gaelic became the language of a
popular church. It was also the medium of a popular
educational movement which created a popular literacy within the Highlands and Hebrides. At the same
time, large numbers of its speakers were being removed from the interior of the Gaelic-speaking area.
Some removed and settled on the coasts but much
larger numbers emigrated to the cities in the south or
emigrated overseas. Some measure of the success of
the Gaelic schools in the promotion of Gaelic literacy
can be gauged from statistics of publications in the
19th century. New titles of Gaelic books from the
commercial press have been counted as follows:-

	Titles
1830-1840	106
1840-1850	164
1850-1860	115
1860-1870	142
1870-1880	169
1880-1890	98
1890-1900	111

Gaelic publishing houses were established and flourished (Norman MacLeod of Edinburgh, Aeneas MacKay of Stirling, Archibald Sinclair and Alexander MacLaren of Glasgow). Also, by the end of the 19th century, Gaelic weekly newspapers were published. *An Gaidheal* (The Gael) in Paisley, and *MacTalla* (The Echo) in Nova Scotia, 1892-1904, (but circulating in Scotland and other Gaelic-speaking centres abroad).

The period was one in which extension of the social uses of Gaelic was conspicuous. Gaelic became the language of the pulpit and religious literature, the medium of popular education, a secular Press and of popular journalism. An important development of folk literature occurred in which popular songs in Gaelic were produced and circulated both within the Highlands and on the concert platforms of societies of Gaelic exiles in Glasgow and other cities. These developments might have continued – as they seem to have done in Wales so far as the Welsh language is concerned – into the twentieth century, assuring for Gaelic a significant role as a national language, a language of a vigorous albeit minority folk life and of a popular literature. Two chief factors which prevented this may be identified in the Clearances and the taking over by a national system of education of the Gaelic schools movement after 1872.

New roles for Gaelic in this period resulted in its use as a medium through which the components of a national culture were being communicated to the Highlanders. The Church in its Gaelic message was accustoming the Gael to the economic necessities of migration or of acceptance of a new social and economic order in his homeland.

Printed literature was familiarising the Highlanders with the ideas and life-styles of an industrial and urban society whose values and culture were in marked contrast to those conveyed by the traditional Gaelic culture then fully extant and popularly enjoyed: Ossianic ballads, sagas, folk tales and chants from the heroic age, work songs and narratives from the medieval period, as well as the productions of the post- medieval popular poets. These poets had been influenced by external literary ideas and models but had generated their work within a pastoral society which by the 19th century, was largely broken up in Gaelic Scotland. S.S.P.C.K. schools had, in some instances, taught industrial processes and technical subjects to the young Gael — presumably as useful knowledge for the industrialisation of his society or as a useful pre-requisite to migration.

Emigration became a persistent feature of Gaelic social conditions. Gaelic colonies in the Carolinas, Cape Breton Island, Nova Scotia, Glengarry (Ontario) and Prince Edward Island received substantial numbers of Gaels throughout the 18th and 19th centuries. In the 20th century, particularly through the merchant navy, large numbers have gone over to the ports of the Commonwealth and Empire as well as to such centres as Boston and Detroit. A hauntingly beautiful popular song which recalls this period of the Gaelic story remains popular today:-

'Gu ma slàn do na fearaibh
Chaidh thairis an cuan,
Gu talamh a' gheallaidh
Far nach fairich iad fuachd,

        'Health to the men
        Who went over the sea,
        To the land of promise
        Where they will no feel the cold,

'Sinn a' fàgail na tir' seo
Oir cha chinnich ann ni dhuinn:
Tha'm bùntàta air dol dhìth oirnn
Is cha chinn iad le fuachd.

        'We are leaving this country
        For nothing will grow for us:
        Potatoes have become scare for us
        And they will not grow for cold.

'Sinn a' fàgail an àit' seo
Bho'n a chuir iad mór mhàl oirnn:
'Nuair a thig an Fhéill Mhàrtainn
Cha bhi nàir air ar gruaidh.

        'We are leaving this place
        Since they put up the rent to us:
        When Martinmas comes
        There'll be no shame on our cheek.

'Gheibh sinn crodh ann is caoraich,
Gheibh sinn cruithneachd air raoin ann,
'S cha bhi'm fearann cho daor dhuinn
'S tha fraoch an taoibh tuath.

        'We'll get cattle and sheep there,
        We'll get wheat on the fields there,
        And land will not be as dear for us
        As heather in the north

'Gu ma slàn do na fearaibh,
Chaidh thairis an cuan.'
    'Health to the men
    Who went over the sea.'

But the song does not tell us just how they fared in
the Nova Scotian winter. The first Highland emi-
grants who sailed in the *'Hector'* to Pictou County in
1773 would have perished in their first winter's snow
but for the help of the local Mic Mac Indians. The
Tiree bard John MacLean later graphically described
in *'A Choille Ghruamach'* ('The Gloomy Forest) the
privations of wresting a living in the harsh climate
and infertile clearings of the Nova Scotian forests.

Gu bheil mi am ònrach 's a' choille ghruamach,
Mo smaointinn luaineach, cha tog mi fonn:
Fhuair mi an t-àit seo an aghaidh nàduir,
Gun thréig gach talanta bha 'nam cheann...

    I'm all alone in this gloomy woodland,
    My mind is troubled, I sing no song;
    Against all nature I took my place here
    And native wit from my mind has gone...

Is i seo an dùthaich 's a bheil an cruadal
Gun fhios do'n t-sluagh a tha tighinnn a nall;
Gur h-olc a fhuaras oirnn luchd a' bhuaraidh
A rinn le an tuairisgeul ar toirt ann...

    This is a country that's hard and cruel,
    They do not know it who journey still;
    Evil the yarns of the smooth-tongued coaxers
    Who brought us hither against our will...

An uair thig an geamhradh is ám na Dùbhlachd
Bidh sneachd a' dlùthadh ri cùl nan geug,
Is gu domhain dùmhail dol thar na glùine,
Is e gu maith triùbhsair cha dèan i feum,

Gun stocainn dhùbailt 's a' mhocais chlùdaich
Bhios air a dùnadh gu dlùth le éill:
B'e am fasan ùr dhuinn a cosg le fionntach
Mar chaidh a rùsgadh de'n bhrùid an dé...

> When comes the winter, and cold December
> The forest branches are clothed in snow,
> No good trousers are defence against it,
> Thigh-deep and thick on the ground below,
> But clouted mocassins and doubled stockings
> And leather thongs are our forest boots:
> Rawhide and fur are our latest fashion
> Lately ripped from the forest brutes...

An uair thig an samhradh 's am miosa Céitein
Bidh teas na gréine ' gam fhàgail fann:
Gun cuir i spéirid ' s a h-uile creutair
A bhois fo éislean air feadh nan toll...

> The month of May and the first of summer,
> My strength is drained by the blazing sun
> That wakes from winter the forst creatures
> Where they lay weakly in den and run...

Chan fhaigh mi àireamh dhuibh ann an dànachd
Gach beathach gràineil a thogas ceann;
Is cho liutha plàigh ann 's a bha air Righ Phàro
Air son nan tràillean 'nuair bhàth e an camp...

> I have not space to relate the boldness
> Of each foul crawler that seeks its prey;
> Like to the plagues that Pharaoh suffered
> My mean condition from day to day...

Iain Mac Ghille-Ethain: AM BARD AN CANADA
Translation by William Neil (adapted).

THE TEACHING-OUT OF GAELIC

From the end of the 19th century, the survival of Gaelic faced its most crucial challenge: the use of the schools to rid society of what was termed by one of Her Majesty's Inspectors of Schools, 'the Gaelic nuisance'. The pressure remained on until after the middle of the present century.

The Education Act (Scotland) 1872 was passed without recognition that the Highlands were an area of particular linguistic significance within a national educational system. No specific references to Gaelic were contained in the Act. The Act set up School Boards in each parish and burgh and to these authorities were transferred all schools set up by parliamentary authority (e.g. the 'Parliamentary' schools set up under an Act of 1838). The boards could purchase private adventure schools, but in the case of Charitable Schools they could only accept and not purchase. The boards thus took over the schools established by the S.S.P.C.K., the General Assembly of the Church of Scotland, the Free Church and the Gaelic Schools Societies. Indeed, these latter had declined in significance since 1841 as charitable moneys had been more readily forthcoming for destitution and famine relief than for education (for which cause the churches were the more successful).

The passing of the 1872 Education Act marks an important turning point for the recognition and use of Gaelic within the education system. Under the new regime, the use of Gaelic was actively discouraged in the schools. The appointment of English-speaking or English teachers was common – as was the punishment of children for speaking Gaelic in schools. The device of the *maide-crochaidh*, a stick on a cord, was commonly used to stigmatise and physically to punish children speaking Gaelic in the schools. Its use is reported as late as the 1930s in Lewis.

Why there should be so sudden a change of policy concerning the use of Gaelic in schools is difficult to appreciate. The agencies promoting public education in the Highlands up to 1872 had been sympathetic to Gaelic and active in its use as a teaching medium. These agencies had readily handed over their educational work to the newly constituted State system. In hindsight, it appears remarkable that they should have done so since, in these respects, the new system proved inimical to the methods and objectives of the schools societies operating within the Gaelic area. Answers may be found in the attitude towards Gaelic of the Scotch Education Department (and its predecessor the Board of Education up until 1878), and the School Boards themselves. These latter were open to

influence of the landed classes which by this time
were English, English-speaking or of Lowland origin
– in any case overwhelmingly anglicised.

The last three decades of the 19th century were not a
period in which the Gaels supinely accepted the adversities of their position in British society. Resistance
to eviction, agitation in the Press and the formation of
associations to promote the welfare of the Highland
people are to be noted. As far as the language is
concerned, in 1871 was established the Gaelic Society
of Inverness which was active in the agitation for the
restoration and advancement of Gaelic within Highland schools and established contacts with M.P's and
H.M.I's to this end. *An Comunn Gaidhealach* (The
Highland Association) was founded in 1891, which
rapidly came to lead the language-loyalty movement,
although it operated chiefly within a Lowland context. Nevertheless, its annual musical and literary
festivals (National and Provincial Mds) became
important foci of Gaelic cultural activity. As an educational pressure group and a publishing agency *An
Comunn* was also considerably more effective than
other Gaelic societies of the time.

As the result of pressures from the Gaelic Society
of Inverness, the Scotch Education Department circulated 102 Highland School Boards in 1876 on the
language question. Ninety replied and of these sixty-
five were in favour of Gaelic teaching and twenty-five
against. Fifty-three boards stated they were able to
provide Gaelic teachers. Two years later, as the result
of a petition organised by the Gaelic Society of Inverness, some permissive provisions favourable to the
inclusion of Gaelic were admitted to the Schools
Code. But by 1881 no real implementation of these

provisions had occurred.

In 1897 the Educational Institute of Scotland gave explicit and strong support to the admission of Gaelic into Highland schools and the Report on the condition of the crofters (The Napier Commission) in 1885 was particularly emphatic in its view of the place of Gaelic in the schools. Inspection through the medium of Gaelic should be enjoined, not merely permitted and knowledge of Gaelic made the primary qualification for every person concerned in public education in Gaelic areas. Despite such authoritative advocacy, Gaelic received no recognition in the Acts of 1892, 1901 and 1908 or in the draft bill of 1918. Only following particular agitation, led by *An Comunn Gaidhealach*, was a mandatory Gaelic clause included in the 1918 Education (Scotland) Act. Even so, the vagueness and brevity of the clause were clearly the chief reasons for its having little effect in promoting Gaelic as a teaching medium in Highland schools.

During this period the role of Gaelic as a teaching medium seems to have been ignored despite the successes which popular education through this medium had already scored. Murdo Macleod, then a Schools Gaelic Supervisor, writing in 1963, observed that notwithstanding the 1918 Gaelic clauses:

'The general pattern in the education of Gaelic-speaking children continued to be one of using Gaelic only when necessity dictated its use. As soon as the Gaelic-speaking pupil had acquired a modest acquaintance with English, Gaelic was almost completely discarded until its study was taken up in a desultory manner in the upper primary classes.'

Scottish public education gave little recognition to

Gaelic language, culture or history – even in the Highlands themselves. The attitude of the central Scottish education authority was one which contained the unspoken assumption that Gaelic was to be replaced as the language of the Highlander. The operation of the explicit policies and assumptions of the writings of James VI and the 17th century educational enactments is clearly a continuing historic tradition – reinforced if anything by the events of the 18th century, and owing a great deal to the ideology of the Whig historians. A similar situation is reported in contemporary Aborigine education schemes in Australia:

'The process of assimilation in Australia is obviously going to mean the extinction of the Australian languages through a guided education which has among its aims the complete transculturation of the native speaker. If he is to take a full part in White Australian life, his own language is more of an obstacle than an advantage ... It will, no doubt, be several generations before the languages disappear ... but they certainly have no future. It is this aspect which has made the Australian government refuse to use the native languages as temporary vehicles of primary education ...' (A. Capell: *Studies in Sociolinguistics*' Mouton 1966)

This seems to have been the case vis-à-vis Gaelic in Scottish education from 1872 at least up until 1918.

The situation quoted by Capell may be contrasted with other types of cross-cultural education ideologies and practices. On the one hand there is a suppressive-alienative model as in the present case; and on the other more liberal models, one of which may be illustrated by the Soviet 'planned culture-contact' schemes in Central Asia, in which vernaculars are cultivated and developed as educational and literary media albeit by an external authority with the aim of encouraging thought and speechways favourable to its regime and which are intended to be ultimately conducive to the acceptance of Soviet culture and the assimilation of the local language. Another typification may be found in the Irish and Welsh systems at the present time where native languages are cultivated and developed as educational and literary media with a view to the replacement of an intrusive language of social dominance. The indifferent results of official policy favouring Irish since independence may be contrasted with the more popular and lively developments centring on Welsh from 1956 – especially since the implementation of the language policies of the Gittins Report.

The Act of 1878 amongst other things attempted to provide for a post-elementary continuation of public education. In the Highlands its effects were delayed owing to the poverty of the microscopic education authorities which reached a financial crisis in the 1880s. By the end of the century a system of Higher Grade and Secondary Schools had come into existence in some of the Highland authorities and a Leaving Certificate Scheme had been introduced in 1888. Examination in Gaelic was not instituted until 1915. Standards were so high that non-Gaelic speakers were deterred from attempting the Gaelic course.

As the road to the professions and to University lay solely through the secondary school this means of social mobility for brighter Gaelic children was more tortuous than for their urban English-speaking contemporaries. Most Gaelic children had at that time to leave home at twelve (or at latest fourteen) and board at a secondary school remote from their homes; a practice that persisted until very recently. Such schools were located in the more anglicised areas. The administrative and teaching media of the school would be English. In terms of language and culture, so too would be the surrounding community. For brighter children then, a process was started at an early age which alienated them from their language and culture. They were then brought to accept an additional move away to college or university even more remote from their home background if they sought professional status.

Gaelic children were perceived as 'disadvantaged' and regarded as 'deficit-systems', in much the same way only perhaps more acutely as slum children 'of poor speech'. No particular benefit was seen in the possession of two languages. Even insofar as Gaelic became a certificate subject after 1915, it did not rank as a 'foreign' or a 'modern' language from the point of Civil Service or professional body entrance requirements, until the 1960s.

Little advantage seems to have been taken of Gaelic children's bilingual ability and bicultural heritage, for example in developing further linguistic proficiencies. Children were to be alienated from their language, and the admission of Gaelic to the curriculum in secondary or academic education can even be regarded as part of this process. The teaching style of these lessons is described in the special report on Education of 1936, compiled by *An Comunn Gaidhealach,* as 'arid, academic and given through the medium of English.'

The school stopped Gaelic as an integral part of the pupil's culture. Alienation of the speakers from their language and culture resulted in the decline of Gaelic as a home language and in the fostering of feelings of inferiority with respect to it. Parents who had come through such an 'educative' process were prepared in their turn further to alienate their children from Gaelic – even to the extent of deliberately using English as a home language. In those parts of the Highlands most open to contact with Lowland society and into which incomers might settle, Gaelic declined as a community language.

In the 20th century the school, an intrusive institution within Gaelic society, became an important agent for change in (or even control of) the social structure of Gaelic Scotland. The school encouraged attitudes towards the native language which ran counter to its maintenance. The school introduced new forms of knowledge into the intellectual life of Gaels which rarely linked up in any coherent way with the surviving elements of their culture. Thus, school subjects, taught through English, came to enjoy prestige and the interpretation of history from English text books generally from an English point of view accepted as received truth (such a pattern of acceptance of the authority of print being noted in regard to the Highlanders' reverence of the Bible).

The traditional lore of Gaelic Scotland, Ossianic and heroic folktales, ballads, folksongs, etc., which may have survived the opposition of the churches in Calvinist areas, enjoyed no great prestige within the community (only the esteem of individuals: the community's own village 'bards' and 'Gaelic scholars'). The village school (elementary/primary and junior secondary) thus alienated the rooted Gaels from their home culture, and acted as a selection agency for the identification of brighter children. The (Senior) secondary school (or 'academy') received these promising children and processed them away from Gaelic society into the core society of modern Britain. Gaelic society thus came to lose its potential community leaders who, for the most part, sought opportunity elsewhere; few openings for their talents existed at home. Gaelic Scotland thus came to lose its intellectual and community-leading individuals (such positions cannot be regarded as collectively forming a 'class' in Gaelic society).

Such individuals, however, were not automatically lost to Gaelic cultural life, as they have been prominent in language-maintenance organisations (e.g. *An Comunn Gaidhealach*, district associations, etc.,) in Lowland centres. They have produced a very large part of the modern literature of Gaelic in the late 19th and throughout the 20th centuries. This last phenomenon illustrates a further method of the social generation of artistic productions and literature: that which Professor Derick Thomson entitles the 'metropolitan'. In this mode the location of the writer or artist is in an urban centre (or at least in strong contact with it) and his or her productions are made specifically for the audience located in such centres. Gaelic publishing became almost entirely centred in Lowland cities and the system of clan and district societies provided large 'concert hall' audiences, particularly in Glasgow. Linguistic and social change has thus brought about a transformation of Gaelic literary culture from the medieval 'high culture' into a 'folk' culture in the early modern period with the superimposition on this 'folk' culture of a minor but nonetheless important 'metropolitan' culture of the later modern period.

Although the literature of this 'metropolitan' culture circulated back into the rooted Gaelic society of the Highlands and Hebrides (notably via such agencies as *An Comunn Gaidhealach* and its *Mods*, commercial recordings and broadcasting), the life of the Gaelic 'colonies' of the Lowlands went ahead as a separate entity from that of the homeland. Gaelic churches and Highland district associations facilitated the maintenance of Gaelic culture and the support of the culture by bonds of fellowship and marriage within the Gaelic group. The use of Gaelic in leisure-time activities posed no particular problem to city Gaels. Their education in the Highlands had ensured that there was no insuperable cultural barrier to their assimilation into the mainstream of British society once they had settled into the cities or out of the Gaelic area. For the most part the Gaels, despite their cultural supports in the city, have followed the route of assimilation into Lowland society.

Within the Gaelic homeland, Gaelic became the language of a residual crofter working-class. As the middle and upper classes within this area consisted of individuals and their families who were for the most part incomers and non-Gaelic in language and culture, we may regard the class structure as one in which anglicised professionals and middle classes were superimposed upon a lower class whose ambitious members were removed into another social setting. The small 'upper class' of landowners, and such surviving clan chiefs as remained in the Gaelic area, was almost entirely English in speech and education.

Thus, in social intercourse across class barriers, Gaelic has had of necessity to give way to English as the incomer population has been conspicuously lacking in interest and proficiency with respect to Gaelic. After all this, it is surprising perhaps that there should have remained any life in the Gaelic speech community at all. But a 'Gaelic problem' still persisted (and was felt particularly in the early stages of infant education).

There was in the mid 20th century even a resurgence of Gaelic as a literary medium, with the poetic work of Sorley MacLean (*Somhairle MacGill-Eain*) and George Caimbeul Hay (*Deòrsa mac Iain Dheòrsa*) in the 1930s and 1940s, notably using new themes, style and poetic forms. The same period saw the development of community drama in Gaelic although the plays were almost entirely translations from Irish, Welsh and English plays. In 1952 the Gaelic quarterly magazine *Gairm* was founded, and introduced – or reintroduced – journalism to Gaelic and popular prose, handling Gaelic and modern subjects of every sort. Through this medium new types of short story in Gaelic have been promoted, and the serialisation of more lengthy prose works of fiction and non-fiction alike.

Since the mid-century a softening of official attitudes towards Gaelic has occurred. A possible explanation of this may lie in the penetration of the educational inspectorate, the bureaucracy of the county education authorities (set up under the 1918 Act) and the Civil Service by intelligent Gaelic speakers. By the 1950s Scottish Education Department memoranda concerning the Primary School and the Junior Secondary School were urging the use of Gaelic as a medium of primary instruction to be followed through with a progressive programme of use and development of work in Gaelic in the successive stages of school. Teachers were encouraged to experiment in the use of Gaelic to teach 'geography, history, music, nature study, rural subjects, home-craft and games'. Experiment the teachers must, for only a literal handful of school texts in and on Gaelic were then in existence. Few of these were well-produced and attractive in appearance.

Three important studies of Gaelic children in Highland Schools were made in the 1930s, 40s and 50s of our present century. They are very revealing of the effects of the 1872 Act.

The first of these studies comprised a special report on education issued by *An Commun Gaidhealach* in 1936 based on questionnaires circulated to schools and education authorities in the Gaelic area. It provides telling evidence of attitudes to Gaelic by parents and teachers. From the west coast of Inverness-shire came the statement:

'The majority of Gaelic-speaking parents are averse to the speaking of Gaelic to their children; they discourage the use of it so that their children have very imperfect English and no Gaelic.' And, 'There exists an animus against the language.' And again, 'The more efficiency I show in teaching Gaelic, the more I am disliked by the parents.' 'Parents object to Gaelic as a waste of time.'

These observations are very likely indicative of attitudes to the language on the part of parents who had internalised the attitudes of their schoolteachers in the previous generation following the 1872 Act.

Teachers observed: 'In a one-teacher school it is

impossible to devote time to Gaelic.' 'With twenty-eight on the roll, a teacher has no time to devote to Gaelic.' 'With sixty-four on the roll and only two teachers, it is impossible to devote time to Gaelic.'

Clearly such teachers felt that with a crowded curriculum Gaelic had to make way for more important work. They did not seem to regard use of Gaelic as a feasible teaching medium. These teachers also had carried forward the official attitudes towards Gaelic from their own schooldays. On the other hand, the use of Gaelic as a teaching medium is reported to be general in infant classes where the pupils were all native speakers. Further up the primary school in such cases its use was confined to Nature Study, Geography, Gardening, Music and History. More extensive use of Gaelic in teaching all subjects at this stage of education was reported at Dunan and Edinbane (Skye) and at Bayble (Lewis), and at Broadford (Skye) extensive use of Gaelic was reported for all subjects throughout the whole school.

A Lewis teacher reported: 'Even parents who are not native speakers are now eager to find their children taking an interest in Gaelic', and adds, 'I am convinced that, where Gaelic is methodically taught, the young speak English with more correctness and fluency than they do when its study is neglected'. The Report added that it was a common testimony from teachers of bilingual children that instead of Gaelic being a hindrance to the acquisition of English it was a help. The Report concluded with some eighteen recommendations urging an extension of the use of Gaelic and improvements in teaching methods in public education, availability of instruction in Gaelic to non-native speakers, the appointment of Gaelic-speakers to administrative posts and improvement of the use and status of the language in Higher Education.

The second of these studies was undertaken in the winter of 1943/44 by Christina A. Smith into the measurement of intelligence in Gaelic and English amongst Gaelic-speaking children in rural Lewis. Her results show up significant cultural differences between Hebridean and mainland/urban children at this time.

Despite the obligatory Gaelic clause of the 1918 Education Act it was quite common throughout the Gaelic-speaking areas, even as late as the 1940s, that Gaelic-speaking children attending State schools were taught in English throughout the entire course of their schooling. Gaelic as a 'specific subject' was a feature of the curriculum in some secondary schools. Typically, then (and even now) the medium of instruction was English. The Scottish Council for Research in Education was in the 1930s aware of the depressed performance in intelligence tests of Gaelic-speaking children and had set up a committee on Bilingualism. Christina A. Smith's research into mental testing in Lewis Schools in 1943/44 and 1945 was its first research enterprise into this problem.

Smith observed that the problem she had studied 'has its genesis in the tacit assumption that Gaelic-speaking Scots form such a small minority that no special administration is needed'. She believes this to be the chief cause of the rapid decline of Gaelic in the 20th century. However, it was conspicuously the case that intelligence tests used with Hebridean children contained much cultural content which was completely alien to the child; circuses, clowns, railway stations, trains, watering cans, trees and garden flowers, sand-castles, lamp-posts, scooters, cricket bats, spinning tops and other toys. More basic cultural differences existed in that the Hebridean child was unused to pictures (still or moving). It must be borne in mind that travelling cinemas were rare in the Hebrides in the 1940's and BBC Medium and Long Wave stations were difficult to receive. Wall-pictures, reading books and comics were largely absent from the children's world and hence even the 'non-verbal' tests, which had been administered (through the medium of English), were imperfectly understood (in the language of instruction), the completion of pictures itself an unfamiliar exercise and the content of the pictures itself utterly strange to the child. Temperamental traits of the Hebridean child such as shyness, reticence, quietness, absence of striving against time (explained as products of Gaelic culture or results of unsureness in using a second language) had also seemed to depress intelligence test scores.

Smith attempted to overcome specifically linguistic factors by translating her tests into Gaelic and comparing scores between tests administered in and through Gaelic with those in which the original English was used. Smith drew attention to the psychological results of the education of infants in an alien language. These, so far as rural Lewis is concerned, were the depression of intelligence-test scores, resulting from the introduction of the second language before literacy and ease of expression had been achieved in the first language, apparent backwardness, aloofness and reticence at school where at the age of five the child had suddenly been introduced into an English only situation. For the rural Lewis child the school was the only social situation (apart from the rare visitor) in which English was used as the medium of communication. It may be the case that the association of English with situations of insecurity and the felt need for defensive behaviour helps to explain the tenacity of Gaelic in the remote areas.

Smith's results and conclusion deserved a more widespread means of publication. Her forty-two page pamphlet suffered from brevity – and hence some lack of clarity in statement of her test results. But she was clear in reporting children's better response when tested in Gaelic, and the unsatisfactory nature of the standard tests then in use. She was somewhat diffident in enunciating reforms which her results seemed to indicate: (1) positive compensatory education to overcome bilingual children's temperamental and environmental deficiencies (2) greater use of Gaelic as a teaching medium in Gaelic-speaking districts (3) educational methods recognising the bilingual child's special advantages (4) postponement of the introduction of English until after the child is at ease in its school (5) teaching reading and writing first in Gaelic (6) revision of means of assessment to recognise the bilinguality of children and their cultural heritage, and the proper matching of test results to those of monolingual and mainland children (7) sympathetic administration by the education authorities. Some ten years elapsed between the publication of Smith's monograph and the introduction of Gaelic education schemes in Inverness-shire (then followed by Ross-shire and later by Argyll).

The Committee on Bilingualism of the Scottish Council for Research in Education was reconstituted

in 1956 and set up further studies of Gaelic bilingualism. Surveys were undertaken of Gaelic-speaking
amongst primary children (especially infants) in 1957
and of first year secondary scholars having knowledge of Gaelic in 1959. The results were published in
1961.

The survey noted not only the general decline in
numbers of speakers of Gaelic recorded in the censuses 1881-1951 and the contraction of the Gaelic-
speaking area but also drew attention to the relatively
greater decline in the incidence of Gaelic within the
younger age-groups. During the period from 1881
onwards the 10-yearly census of Scotland has sought
information as to the ability to speak Gaelic amongst
the population aged three years and over. In 1881
231,594 persons claimed 'habitually' to speak Gaelic
(out of a Scottish population of 3,425,151 aged three
years or over). By 1951 Gaelic speakers had declined
to 95,447 (out of 4,826,814) and by 1961 to 80,978
(out of 4,892,882). As a percentage these numbers
correspond to 6.76% of the population of Scotland as
'habitually' Gaelic-speaking in 1881, 6.84% Gaelic-
speaking in 1891, 1.98% in 1951 and 1.66% in 1961.

The Gaelic-speaking area in the period 1881/1891
extended throughout the Highlands and Hebrides.
The percentage of Gaelic speakers dropped below
50% only in Caithness, urban areas around the
Moray Firth and the extreme eastern and southern
margins of the Grampians, the south end of Kintyre,
eastern Arran and Bute. However, by 1951 considerable contraction had occurred. The 50%+ Gaelic-
speaking area then enclosed only the western margins
of Sutherland and Ross-shire, excluding Lochalsh
and including only the peninsular area of western

Inverness-shire and north Argyll between Lochs Morar and Sunart. The Hebrides remained within this 50% + area with the exception of northern and eastern Mull.

Amongst school children the two surveys of this study indicated a pronounced decline of Gaelic amongst the younger age groups. In infant departments in 1957 there were 941 children whose first language was Gaelic (0.5% of this age-group in Scotland). The total of primary aged children whose first or preferred language was Gaelic was 3,829 (or 0.6% of all Scottish primary children). Amongst first year secondary-aged children in the Highland area in 1959 those with some degree of claimed knowledge of Gaelic was 908 (or 1.2% of the total Scottish year-group). The downward trend of the ability to speak Gaelic is clear from these figures but two points must be borne in mind:-

(1) The figures represent a more rigorous definition of ability to speak Gaelic than does the official census.

(2) The survey does not account for Gaelic-speaking children outside the principal bilingual area. There are parents who maintain Gaelic as the home language despite migration to a non-Gaelic-speaking area.

It may be argued that the sporadic occurrence of Gaelic speech outside the recognisable Gaelic-speaking area is of little significance to the statistics of language in the Gaelic community. However, there have been increasingly important social influences upon the Gaelic home community from exiles in the Lowlands. Persons active in Gaelic-language movements have included such people of two cultures as the late Lord Bannerman who was born and brought up in a working-class area of Glasgow of Gaelic-speaking parents at the turn of the century. As with children from Gaelic areas, he also claimed not to have learned English until entering primary school. However, the secondary school survey of the study 'Gaelic-speaking children in Highland Schools' did note the situation where Gaelic was taught as a secondary school subject outside the Highlands in such city schools as Bellahouston Academy and Woodside Senior Secondary (Glasgow) since 1946, Greenock High School and Norton Park (Edinburgh) both since 1958. Of a total of 89 first year pupils taking Gaelic as a specific subject in these schools, Gaelic was the first language of six pupils. Pupils with English as their first language claimed 'fair fluency' in Gaelic, six cases claimed 'fair fluency', 62 claimed to 'understand simple lessons' and could 'conduct elementary conversation in Gaelic.' This would seem to be an impressive achievement of success for the first year of study of a new foreign language. The survey pointed out that these children taking Gaelic are not as a rule children of Gaelic-speaking parents. Bellahouston Academy also organised six periods of Gaelic per week in its primary department. (From 1952 there had been Saturday morning Gaelic classes for nursery aged children at the Highlanders' Institute, Glasgow, and for primary school ages at Glasgow Boys' High School.)

The survey of Gaelic-speaking children in Highland schools also sought to investigate the social use of language and the social distribution of language within its field.

Concerning the relationship of language and occu-

pation the survey sets out the numbers and percentages of children in the first two years of primary
school in the bilingual area of Argyll, Inverness and
Ross-shire whose parents' occupations fall within
seven status-ranked categories. (The bilingual area is
defined as the area whose schools contain at least 8%
of their children able to speak Gaelic.) The totals are
interesting to note, and I have later added a table
which brings out these proportions in terms of percentages.

Occupational Class of Parent	Totals of children of first language:		% of Total First language:	
	Gaelic	English	Gaelic	English
A. Professional	13	40	1	6
B. Civil/Public Servants	26	63	3	10
C. Commercial	32	111	4	17
D. Technical	181	162	20	24
E. Agriculture, Forestry	354	129	39	19
F. Manual workers	115	70	13	10
G. Unemployed	117	95	20	14

The survey is cautious in interpreting this data but
the survey noted that there were proportionately
more of categories A,B and C in the English group.
The Survey was not correct in stating that for both
English and Gaelic groups Category E (Agriculture,
Forestry, Crofting) was numerically the most important. This is so for Gaelic children, but for the English
group the largest occupational category was D (skilled
technical occupations). Gaelic, however, predominated over English as the first language of the 'lower'
status occupational groups taken as a whole from D
(Technicians) 'downwards'. The ratios of first-language Gaelic to first-language English children ex-

pressed as percentages of each occupational category
may be derived as follows:-

Occupational Class of Parents	% of Primary I and Primary II children whose first language was	
	Gaelic	English
A. (professional)	75.5	24.5
B. (public servants)	70.8	29.2
C. (commercial)	77.6	22.4
D. (technical)	47.2	52.8
E. (agricultural)	26.7	73.3
F. (manual)	37.8	62.2
G. (unemployed)	44.8	55.2

It can be seen that the incidence of Gaelic as a first
language of these primary schoolchildren is in fact
somewhat weaker amongst the two 'lowest' status
occupational groups: F (manual) and G (unemployed) than it is amongst children of occupational
group E (agricultural). It would be tempting to suggest from these figures that language-loyalty is greatest amongst the crofter-agricultural occupational
group than amongst the occupational groups of
higher or lower social prestige. However, these figures are not in themselves sufficient data to point to
such a general conclusion and the broadness of the
occupational categories might very well obscure occupational groupings at either end of the scale which
might provide evidence of the highest degrees of
language-loyalty and language-maintenance as perhaps do ministers of religion and nomadic 'tinker'
families (*na cèardan*). The connection between lang-

uage and occupational grouping to which the survey draws attention must be a complex one. There are probably at least three factors at work:-

(1) An incoming movement of professional, clerical, commercial, skilled technical and some at least of manual workers who are English monoglots from outwith the Gaelic area;

(2) A shift in favour of English from Gaelic as a home language on the part of 'educated' Gaelic speakers entering the 'higher' status groups and continuing in or returning to the Gaelic area;

(3) A mixed-marriage situation where a non-Gaelic spouse ensures that English becomes the language of the home.

In this latter case the incidence probably operates to different degrees in the various categories so that it is the potential occupants of occupational groups A, B, C and D who may leave the Gaelic area to train elsewhere and return with a non-Gaelic spouse. This whole social situation deserved much closer study than this or any other any census or survey of this problem had so far been able to give it. Considerable assumptions have been made about this problem by Gaels themselves, public opinion in Scotland generally, official policy and administrative agencies.

The survey of Gaelic-speaking children also attempted to investigate the use of the language in various aspects of the children's lives; in the home, with one parent or both, with brothers and sisters, in the playground, with other children, to the teacher, as a medium of school instruction, religious worship and community life. This report was particularly interesting at the time as it had been the only serious study of the social use of Gaelic to date. The figures

gave interesting and penetrating insights into the
nature of Gaelic-English bilingualism and the social
roles undertaken using the medium of Gaelic speech
in the various local communities of the Gaelic-speaking area in the late 1950's.

The survey calculated that within the bilingual
area: 'It will be found that of all the homes where
both parents are Gaelic-speaking, only in 50% of
those in Argyll is the language of the home Gaelic.
The percentages for Inverness-shire and Lewis are
91% and 80% respectively.'

The survey further concluded that: 'As the child
moves out from the Gaelic-speaking home, the tendency is for English to appear more and more as the
language in the specific situation, the only exception
to this is the strong Gaelic communities where Gaelic
is spoken in the playground, and where the English-
speaking child is under some pressure to speak Gaelic
... It will be noted that even in the strongest Gaelic-
speaking communities, the language spoken to the
teacher is almost invariably English. This accords with
what has already been discovered about the usual
medium of instruction in infant classes in Highland
schools. The English-speaking child, on the whole,
whether he (sic) is living in an English community or a
Gaelic one, speaks English in any situation. The
Gaelic- speaking child speaks Gaelic naturally to his
(sic) sisters and brothers, Gaelic as a rule to the other
children and in the playground except in the more
anglicised areas, but English to his (sic) teacher except
when he is encouraged to speak in Gaelic.'

It may be surprising that after over ten years following Smith's work on the mental testing of children
in Lewis that it is reported that: 'Teaching in infant

departments is given mainly through the medium of English, whether the children are Gaelic-speaking or English-speaking ... In nearly all cases the teacher herself is Gaelic-speaking although she teaches in English.'

This situation changed considerably in the years following the survey as county advisers for Gaelic were appointed, and attitudes towards Gaelic improved within the schools. For example, in Harris, where the reported absence of Gaelic from half its primary schools in 1957 was certainly not the case by the early '70s with Gaelic being in general use in the infant classes – often in sole use.

The survey described the process of anglicisation within the Gaelic-speaking area of the Hebrides as follows: 'The process of anglicisation begins historically around the official centres of transport on the east side of the island opposite the mainland. Thereafter, an English 'pale' develops inland from the bridge or pierhead. It may be some time before the development makes any marked advance inland. This is still true of Stornoway in Lewis (it is also true of Tarbert (Harris), Lochmaddy (North Uist), Lochboisdale (South Uist), and Castlebay (Barra). In Skye, on the other hand, as can be seen around Portree and Kyleakin, the development once begun soon spreads. Before the 'breakthrough' occurs there are signs of the times to be seen here and there. What happens is that localities, such as Elgol in Skye at the present time, that were traditionally Gaelic, tend to become anglicised for various local reasons, and then the whole front proceeds to break up. That process is now nearing completion in Mull and Islay.'

OLD STOCK,
NEW SHOOTS

'Thalla, Eudochais, is beachdaich.
   A' chraobh a leag iad an uiridh –
seall! – cha n-fhaic thu 'stoc am bliadhna
   aig lionmhorachd nam fiùran uime....

'Ar cainnt 's ar cultur, car sealain
   ged rachadh an leagadh buileach,
cuiridh am freumhan 's an seann stoc dhiubh
   failleanan snodhaich is duilleach.'

Deòrsa Caimbeul Hay: STOC IS FAILLEANAN

'Come, Despondency, gaze on this sign and ponder.
   The tree they felled in the year that is gone
look! seek for the stump – this Spring you cannot find it
   for the young shoots around it so close they have grown..
'Our speech and culture – Despondency, consider -
   though they be brought low for a time and forgotten by men,
the old stock still has its roots, and the roots they will bring us
   shoots and sap, branches and leaves again.'

George Campbell Hay: *OLD STUMP AND YOUNG SHOOTS*

These verses were first published in 1948 and were probably composed during or shortly after the Second World War. The prospects for Gaelic were scarcely at a lower ebb. Any place or support for Gaelic came nowhere in the priorities for postwar social and economic reconstruction. Attitudes towards the language were instrumental: there was still a 'Gaelic problem'.

Children were still being raised in the language and needed educating out of it. Its maintenance and culture were matters only for private or scholarly concern. Its speakers and supporters were deferential in any case they made for the language – almost to the point of apology: putting their case in others' terms, not their own. Yet the poet had confidence and vision. Reading the verses at the time, I pondered to myself, 'If only...!' Over forty years on I have lived to see much of his confidence fulfilled.

The census returns for 1951 and 1961 produced yet further downturns in the spiral of decline of the language. Numbers of speakers dropped from 136,135 to 95,447 between 1931 and 1951, and again to 80,978 in 1961. But by 1971 numbers rose by almost 10% to 88,892, and although there was a relapse to 79,307 of speakers, or to 82,620 of all users of Gaelic in 1981, these last two censuses evidenced for the first time ever a growth in numbers of Gaelic speakers amongst school-age children and young people, and in 1981 the first ever increase in numbers in core Gaelic areas such as the Western Isles. Throughout the 1940s and for much of the '50s, the place of Gaelic in education, the media and in public life generally was muted and vestigial but change was on its way and its pace was to accelerate.

The recent situation was preceded by two developments of considerable significance for the social use of Gaelic. These developments were of opposite influence to one another in the processes of language maintenance. By the end of the 1950s the virtual disappearance from the Gaelic-speaking community of a significant body of monoglot Gaelic-speakers had come. In 1958 Gaelic-medium education schemes were introduced into the primary schools of the remaining bilingual areas of Inverness-shire subsequently followed in Ross-shire and in some measure in Argyll.

Of the 974 persons enumerated in the 1961 census as speaking Gaelic only, 406 were in the age-group 3-4 and 100 in the age- group 5-9 and hence should be regarded as potential learners of English. Of persons aged 65 and over, 309 represented the core of surviving Gaelic monolingualism and of this number only 65 were males.

It has been questioned whether, in the case of a minority language in decline, the language can long survive the disappearance of its last monoglot speakers. Saunders Lewis, the Welsh writer and nationalist politician observed of Welsh that: 'Soon after the monoglot speakers of Welsh have disappeared the language will die. For then it will be vain to talk of the spiritual and educational value of Welsh. It will not be a necessity for living in Wales, and when it will no longer be necessary anywhere, then it will collapse everywhere.'

His broadcast of 1962, given in Welsh and entitled *Tynged yr Iaith* (The Fate of the Language), had a galvanising effect on the language movement in Wales, bringing about the formation of such radical and militant groups as the Welsh Language Society, the Adfer housing trust and others which secured publicity, action, and official recognition and use of Welsh in Wales. Nothing like this has so far happened in Scotland. Welsh writers like Gerald Morgan believe it possible as 'the compactness of the Gaelic-speaking area would make a campaign quite feasible'.

In criticism of such an extreme and pessimistic view as that of Saunders Lewis, evidence from the sociology of language may be brought forward of numerous instances of persistence within bilingual communities of separate languages in which different social roles are communicated. Whatever is to be the future pattern of Gaelic-English bilingualism in Scotland, the social situation whereby Gaelic has of necessity to be used to convey information within the adult speech community has now passed. Gaelic monolingualism in Scotland is not a feature of communities or even of families; it was by the 1960s a feature of a small number of isolated, and in the main elderly people – chiefly women. Gaelic continues to have a variety of roles: in worship, in entertainment, in social life, communication amongst the crowd at public events (shearings, 'fank days', agricultural shows, games, etc.).

Such uses might be described as the expressive or affective aspects of social life. Even within the Gaelic area it was rare for Gaelic to be used by platform speakers at public events, in political meetings, in business life (except for individual buying and selling in shops and the like), in any form of official communication, public advertisement or written sign, in council or committee meetings (until the formation of *Comhairle nan Eilean* in 1975). The instrumental aspects of social life are, and in modern times in large measure always have been, communicated through the English language. Hence it would not be inconceivable that some persistence of Gaelic speech may occur well after the passing of effective monolingualism whilst there remains some perceived need or preference to handle certain important aspects of social life through the medium of Gaelic. The present situation is one in which this state of affairs may be said to be perpetuating itself.

The introduction of Gaelic as a medium of instruction into the county primary schools in the bilingual area from 1958 was the first in a number of changes in attitude and policy towards the language by public authorities. That this improvement of attitudes towards Gaelic occurred at a time when the problem of public communication in the Highlands may be said to be solved, might be coincidental or casually connected. Romantic Jacobitism had, for example, become a fashionable fad once the political and military Jacobite threat to Lowland society had collapsed and died. In like manner the Gaelic Education Scheme might be argued to be a preservationist move by the Education Authorities whose chief work, the universal promotion of the knowledge of spoken and written English, had been accomplished. Alternatively a latent function of the scheme might be that of more effective assimilation of English by the schoolchildren resulting from their introduction to literacy occurring through the medium of the more familiar mother-tongue of their homes. However, the inception of this scheme marks a turning point for the relationship of Gaelic and the public authorities. In the following year a number of other now official policies might be regarded as now positively contributing to more favourable circumstances for the language.

In broadcasting, Gaelic programmes on the Scottish Home Service (Radio 4) increased from some two hours weekly in 1959 to about three hours in 1967 and to almost four hours weekly by 1970. Unfortunately, from January 1971 the BBC reduced its weekly output in Gaelic to between 2¼ and 2¾ hours. The Gaelic minority might be said to be entitled to between 8 and 10 hours weekly as a proportion of total broadcast time. The BBC claimed to broadcast 3½ hours weekly but this was not factually the case.

The BBC also claimed to broadcast and to spend on behalf of its Gaelic public in greater proportion than their numbers in the population, as a whole, would justify. Assuming Gaelic programmes were not significantly more expensive to produce, the computation of the proportion of broadcast time devoted to Gaelic hardly supported this claim. By the end of the 1960s a short weekly Gaelic musical programme was being broadcast on BBC TV Scotland as well as a monthly current affairs programme and occasional Gaelic services and plays.

Improvements in the financial support of *An Comunn Gaidhealach*, then the principal language promotional organisation, by Government and local authorities and others, enabled it to appoint a professional director and a full time public relations officer in 1965. In the same year the Highlands and Islands Development Board was established which, through its social grants, has given some assistance to Gaelic publishing and promotional events. Government subsidy and charitable trust contributions enabled a historical dictionary to be commenced by Glasgow University (1966); and in 1969 the passage of the Local Authorities (National *Mòd*) Bill in Parliamentary time made available by the Government enabled Scottish local authorities who wished to do so to provide financial aid for the National *Mòd*. The Government had already promised annual sums of money for the subsidisation of Gaelic books and in 1969 the Gaelic Books Council was established under the aegis of the Glasgow University Celtic Department. Prior to its establishment some two or three new Gaelic titles were being published annually, and in its first full year of operation it had stimulated 37 new titles (including reprints).

Schools broadcasting in Gaelic commenced early in 1970. The previous Labour administration was prepared to sanction and to admit for subsidy the use of Gaelic on road signs but this was only taken up by a few district authorities for village signs. The incoming Conservative government in 1970 stated through the new Secretary of State for Scotland that it intended to maintain and strengthen these new policies for Gaelic. In 1970 improving financial support of *An Comunn Gaidhealach* enabled it to appoint a deputy Director for its work in the Western Isles. The Highland Book Club (*Club Leabhar*) commenced its first issues in 1970. It produced six/seven titles each year in Gaelic, English and bilingually over about ten years. The English titles subsidised the Gaelic publications. *An Comunn* published a bilingual fornightly newspaper *Sruth* between 1965-69.

Impatience with the slowness of results from the existing Gaelic Societies led to the establishment in 1971 of *Comunn na Cànain Albannaich,* modelled on the Welsh Language Society and desirous of copying its methods of militant non-violent civil disobedience. However in practice it functioned more as 'think-tank', opening up new issues for public debate.

During the '60s, Gaelic became the first language of instruction in the infant classes of the bilingual area. It also became a medium of instruction for subjects other than religious education throughout the primary stage and the language of the Gaelic periods at least in the older primary and junior secondary schools. In the senior secondary schools academic education was handled through the medium of English almost entirely, Gaelic being taught even to Gaelic-speaking children in English! There were two senior secondary schools within the bilingual area (the Nicolson Institute, Stornoway, Lewis, and Portree High School, Skye). Some five or six other senior secondary schools served the bilingual area: Lochaber High School, Inverness High School and Inverness Royal Academy (Inverness-shire), Dingwall Academy (Ross-shire), Dunoon High School and Oban High School (Argyllshire). Each of these schools has published yearly magazines with a good selection of Gaelic items.

There was a shift away from traditional methods in the Gaelic classroom. Modern methods were introduced to teach reading through the medium of Gaelic. As the subject continued into older primary and junior secondary stages there came to be a move away from a formal concern with the insistence on the intricacies of traditional Gaelic spelling and punctilious adherence to traditional grammatical forms, which are moribund in everyday speech, and precise translations into English.

Instead, project work and comprehension have replaced the formal and abstract unfavourable attitudes towards the language amongst schoolchildren. In Shawbost, Lewis, a very successful series of projects in technical subjects in the Junior Secondary School was allied to the restoration of local industrial archaeology (a 'Norse'-type mill), involving Gaelic technical terms and the provision of a village museum in which the history and contemporary life of the village is annotated in Gaelic as well as English. Research has also been undertaken into Gaelic place-names for the School of Scottish Studies Edinburgh University by junior secondary schools in Harris together with projects on the local Harris tweed industry, folk medicine and the like. There is a danger in this type of work that Gaelic may come to be identified exclusively with traditional folk life and that work on old mills, collections of village bygones and traditional cures will only serve to link Gaelic in the minds of the children with a way of life which is superseded – or at the best moribund. Schools radio programmes in Gaelic (started early in 1970) have been some corrective as they have featured new developments in fishing, navigation, agriculture and industry.

In Inverness-shire Gaelic was introduced as a second language into mainland primary schools including the Inverness area itself. This development proved to be popular and the language became part of the curriculum in about two-thirds of the authority's mainland schools. In 1962 Gaelic was introduced at Higher and Ordinary grades of the S.C.E. for learners.

The situation prior to local government reorgan-

isation in 1975 had been marked by a more sympathetic and liberal attitude towards the language by
public authorities generally. Gaelic education
schemes operated in the Gaelic areas at primary
school level but academic education was still typically
in English and remote from the home. The junior
secondary schools in the home areas had however,
extended the uses of Gaelic as a school language. A
new literate generation of young Gaelic-speaking
adults had come through the schools since 1958.
This, coming after an important Gaelic literary revival, had implications for the strengthening of those
elements of Gaelic culture which were viable. The
survival of Gaelic into the present day as the spoken
language of a tenacious folk community and its cultivation as a literary medium drawing from native and
outside sources may be regarded as an achievement
deserving encouragement and support.

Survival and adaptations have occurred in the face
of persistent adverse circumstances over a long period. Hence the explanation of the persistence of
Gaelic language and culture as a case of 'cultural lag'
is not at all adequate. This study must now turn to a
consideration of what explanations may account for
the survival of Gaelic as community speech and the
processes of language-maintenance and language-
loyalty associated with them.

PART 2: ISSUES

RECOGNITION

The legal or official status of Gaelic is contentious to say the least. It may be argued as having no officially recognised status – or having always enjoyed it, needing no specific legislation to regularise its position. 'Having it both ways' means that officialdom can always fall back on a contrary argument to justify its position. It is an official principle at least as old as

'Morton's Fork'. This has happened to Gaelic in a number of ways.

In the wake of the Welsh roadsigns campaign of the 1960's, the Gaelic Society of London decided to lobby parliamentarians and government departments, as it was well placed to do so, over a number of current Gaelic issues – including bilingual signs. In 1969/70 the official position of the Scottish Office (2.4.69) was that use of Gaelic on signs was entirely within the discretion of local authorities and not a matter for the Secretary of State. The Scottish Home and Health Department (22.4.70) however later observed: 'if a good case can be made out by a local authority...this could be dealt with by...the Secretary of State's powers of special authorisation.' Subsequent correspondence confirmed that bilingual signs would rank for grant as any others. In circularising sixty-four Highland and Island county and district authorities in 1970, the Society received replies from twenty-eight. Stornoway stated that it was existing policy, and seven districts adopted the policy and some at least, in Sutherlandshire, implemented it.

Arguments such as 'minimal benefit', 'who is to pay for them?' and 'non-essential' were made – but the replies of Inverness-shire and Perthshire were interestingly contrasted. The Divisional Road Surveyor for Badenoch felt that bilingual signs would cause traffic to stop and add to congestion on the trunk road. (21.7.70) The Perth County Roads Surveyor believed that the 'proportion of tourists who would benefit would be minimal'. (23.7.70) The most negative replies were forthcoming from the Inverness-shire district authorities – a number replying in identical phraseology, indicating some measure of co-ordinated policy. The intransigence of the county highways authority was manifested again a decade later over the roadsigns issue in Skye.

In 1972 the county authority requested easements for road improvements in the Isle of Skye from the local laird. Iain Noble of *Fearann Eilean Iarmain* replied that the land would be conveyed free providing three Gaelic signs were erected on the improvement in addition to the English ones. The Inverness-shire highways authority dug its heels in, and over a year later was still contending that this request was holding up much needed improvements. (The county could of course easily have gone for compulsory purchase – or saved this and much else expense in readily agreeing the signs.) The county surveyor, Keith MacFarlane, came out strongly in public statements against the principle of bilingual signs on grounds of road safety, and Lord Burton, the highways convener on grounds of lack of public debate (West Highland Free Press 16.3.73). But the authority eventually conceded with two of the signs: Broadford being additionally signed *An t-Ath Leathann*, and *Goirtean na Créige* replacing Viewfield Road on the outskirts of Portree. Skye was to be the arena for further developments over this issue.

In 1975 the new structures of local government came into being, and the Western Isles Islands Area acted very swiftly in adopting bilingual policies in administration as well as in primary edcuation. The council took as an official title *Comhairle nan Eilean* – the historic name of the deliberative assembly of the medieval Lordship of the Isles. Within a few years, simultaneous translation facilities were installed in the new council chamber, with Gaelic becoming the language used in a number of its committees and debates, bilingual signing became general on the council's own premises and vehicles, and Gaelic place-names became officially adopted. Roadsigns indicating placenames thus became monolingual in Gaelic – and by 1980 this had led to a controversy over their intelligibility. Meanwhile, the situation in Skye as the other main Gaelic-speaking area remained pretty well the status quo.

In 1980, Donald Stewart, the SNP leader in the Commons, was fortunate in the ballot to introduce a private member's bill. Legislation on behalf of Gaelic had been advocated by the campaigns of the Gaelic Society of London and *Comunn na Cànain Albannaich* since the early '70s. Donald Stewart's Gaelic (Miscellaneous Provisions) Bill sought to do three things: give legal recognition to Gaelic, define the 'Gaelic-speaking areas' in which the 1918 Education Act had enjoined Gaelic instruction in schools, and to set up broadcasting and television facilities for Gaelic on the Welsh pattern. On Friday 13th February 1981 the bill was talked out in a four hour filibuster organised by the government whips who had put the bill on the order paper immediately before a measure introduced by a Welsh Nationalist M.P. to bring slate quarriers under similar industrial health provisions to miners. The device was deliberately arranged so that the industrial injuries compensation bill was not even reached – and no Conservative M.P. need be identifiable in saying 'object' in order to kill it.

The leading speakers in taking up the time of the house to talk out the Gaelic Bill were Douglas Hogg (Grantham) and Bill Walker (Perth East). Many of their arguments were specious, incorrect and pro-

vocative. They, and the then M.P. for Argyll and
Bute, John MacKay offended many of the Gaelic-
speakers present in the visitors' gallery and the stewards had on occasion to quieten their reactions and
the laughter at outright nonsense. The result of the
Bill's failure was to prompt a civil disobedience
campaign undertaken by a number of clandestine, ad
hoc, pro-Gaelic groups, the most effective being *Cear-
tas* ('Justice') and *Stri* ('Struggle'). In the following
weeks these groups undertook roadsign defacement
on Welsh lines in Skye, Perthshire and Lochaber.

The issue culminated at a weekend conference on
the status of Gaelic at *Sabhal Mòr Ostaig*, the Gaelic
college in Sleat in May 1981. The then principal Iain
Taylor and Steaphan MacEachainn, another fulltime
worker at the college, publicly tore up the census
forms they had refused to complete as they had not
been provided in Gaelic. Daubing of local roadsigns
took place that night, to be followed by campaigns in
Skye and other areas. Later that year, all the roadsigns bearing the words Fort William along the A82
road from outside Glasgow to the venue of the Lochaber *Mòd* were unofficially changed on the night
before the official opening ceremony for properly
painted signs bearing the words *An Gearasdan*. This
action was described by the local chief constable and
Mòd convener, who had previously warned off the
'daubers', as 'a professional job'.

Iain Taylor made public his involvement in the
Skye roadsign defacements and was eventually ar-
rested and charged with painting out the English
wording of the Skye Airstrip sign and spray-painting
the words *Port Adhair* in their place on 4th May 1981.
An attempt was clearly under way to emulate the

tactic of the Welsh 'language-trials' which had been precipitated by similar roadsign activity – and there was some delay before the matter came to court. The panel was clearly going to insist on Gaelic being used at the trial and a test-case was obviously about to be set up.

The official position of Gaelic in law had been that no legislation was necessary, as unlike Welsh before 1967 it was officially regarded as having equal validity with English. A libel case in the mid-19th century hinging upon defamations published in Gaelic had tacitly recognised the language, and there had been no Act of Parliament such as the 1536 Act of Union between England and Wales which had legislated that no persons using the Welsh speech should have any office or fees in Wales unless they used English and that any business would have no legal effect unless transacted in English. Correspondence from the then Secretary of State (Gordon Campbell, 10.7.70) and previously from the Scottish Office (2.4.69) to the Gaelic Society of London enunciated the principles that, 'There is nothing in the law of Scotland to prevent a witness testifying in Gaelic and the Secretary of State is not aware of any case in which the Court has refused to hear evidence in that language'; and, 'There are in fact no explicit statutory limitations on the use in official or legal matters of the Gaelic language which enjoys equal validity with English'. The case was significantly to modify and correct these principles in practice.

Iain Taylor's trial took place at Portree Sheriff Court on 14th April 1982 before Sheriff Scott Robinson. Iain Taylor identified himself in Gaelic and replied in Gaelic when questioned on his plea.

Application was then made for the trial to be conducted in Gaelic. The Sheriff ordered the trial to
proceed in English, whereupon Iain Taylor's solicitor, Mr. Donald Ferguson, moved an appeal, which
was heard on 16th June 1982 by Lord Justice-Clerk
Wheatley and Lords Hunter and Dunpark. The sheriff's decision was upheld and reference was made to
the case of Alexander McRae in 1841 whose request
to give evidence in Gaelic was similarly refused on the
grounds that 'the witness could speak English 'with
perfect distinctness'. Thus the request on Iain Taylor's behalf that he might identify himself, take the
oath, and address the court in Gaelic, and that its
proceedings be translated into Gaelic was on appeal
refused.

The law of Scotland thus has it both ways. Gaelic is
recognised insofar as anything said or written in it
could have competent legal effect. A witness in-
capable of speaking English can be heard and the
testimony translated. In making the point to Sherriff
Robinson that 'the language of the criminal courts of
Scotland had from time immemorial been English..',
Andrew Haughney, the Portree Procurator Fiscal,
carefully avoided the fact that in the Scottish Land
Court Gaelic has always been perfectly acceptable as
the language of the court, and legislation requires the
court always to have a Gaelic-speaking member. In
accepting the fiscal's principle, Sheriff Robinson was
also careful to modify the description of the language
used to: 'the Scots vernacular or in more modern
times... English'.

What has been overlooked in this issue is the fact
that although there are very few persons today for
whom it would be instrumentally necessary to trans-

late from English into Gaelic, there are many Gaelic speakers who feel more at ease in Gaelic than English. If the courts were to make ready provision for them, many Gaelic speakers would nevertheless choose to speak in English since in their view to speak in Gaelic might be held to reflect poorly upon their linguistic competence and self-pride. The Welsh situation whereby Welsh-speaking courts enable Welsh-speakers, whatever their competence in English, to use their language naturally and without special arrangements for translation would merely be an extension of what exists already in the Scottish Land Court (which could well have been a precedent for Wales). In July 1984 a witness was not allowed to speak in Gaelic at Inverness Sherriff Court without proof of deficiency in English.

It may also have been a mistake for a fluent English-speaker such as Iain Taylor to request a translation of the court proceedings from English into Gaelic. If we do not yet have Gaelic-speaking Sheriff Courts, a reasonable way-stage might be a bilingual Sheriff Court in which Gaelic-speakers, whatever their competence in English, might speak in Gaelic with the translation – from Gaelic into English – being provided for those who did not understand it. It would be the court, rather than the panel, that would need the translator. The Taylor case might have thus have drawn more effective attention to the lack of a Gaelic- speaking judiciary within the *Gàidhealtachd*.

There had been at this time some modest advance for Gaelic in legal recognition, and reference was made to it by Donald Ferguson, Iain Taylor's defending solicitor. The 1981 Nationality Act recognised Gaelic, together with English and Welsh, as one of the

qualifying indigenous languages of the United Kingdom which an applicant for British citizenship must
be able to speak. In the House of Commons debate on
19th October 1971 on the previous Nationality Act,
the moves to include Welsh (and on a question from
Merlyn Rees other languages including Gaelic)
turned on the desirability of immigrants being able to
speak English as the language of general communication in the United Kingdom. The upshot was to include Welsh as it had some official status in at least
part of the United Kingdom, and according to Enoch
Powell, although absurd, had to be accepted 'for the
sake of a quiet life'. Merlyn Rees pointed out that
there were countries such as Canada where Gaelic, as
an indigenous language of Scotland was spoken, and
on these grounds should also be recognised.

One of the indirect effects of Donald Stewart's
unsuccessful Gaelic Bill may have been to assist the
inclusion of Gaelic as a qualifying British language in
the Nationality Bill going through Parliament later in
1981.

The spirit of this act was to restrict further the
grounds for claiming British citizenship and the debate was not so acutely directed to problems of immigrants making themselves understood at work. The
Gaelic Society of London convened a meeting in the
Royal Scottish Corporation Hall on Shrove Tuesday.
Various parliamentarians attended including a
government member, Hamish Gray (Ross and Cromarty). Perhaps he was there in some measure of
exculpation for the government's shabby treatment
of Donald Stewart's bill – or to monitor an issue over
which the government was concerned as it entered a
post-election sag in popularity. Anyway, he was put

on the spot after addressing the meeting, and promised that Gaelic would receive some measure of justice in the next parliamentary session.

It can therefore be shown that Gaelic has been recognised in legislation in various ways, although they can be counted on the fingers of one hand: the 'Gaelic Clause' of the 1918 Education Act, legislation setting up the Scottish Land Court and the Crofter's Commission whereby both must have at least one Gaelic-speaking member, Russell Johnston's Local Authorities (National *Mòd*) Act 1969, and the 1981 Nationality Act. It is difficult to think of any other legislation recognising Gaelic in any specific way.

There have however been some developments for Gaelic undertaken by the Secretary of State, government departments and quangos which have greatly improved the prospects for the language. Some have been crucially significant. Looking back from the early '90's, it is surprising how many of the measures have been achieved which Gaelic pressure groups such as *An Comunn Gàidhealach,* the Gaelic Society of London, and *Comunn na Cànain Albannaich* were advocating in the '60s and '70s, and what progress had been made with others – yet the unequivocal definition of legal status and official recognition for Gaelic still remains unresolved.

In its early years, the Highlands and Islands Development Board, established by a Labour government in 1964, had been criticised for not fulfilling its social remit or giving specific recognition or assistance to Gaelic. Its first chairman Professor Robert Grieve had said that it was the role of the Board to bring people jobs, and the task of *An Comunn Gàidhealach* to put Gaelic in people's mouths. It is doubtful whether such a simplistic view would be officially enunciated today. In the late '70s the Board did however commence a policy of promoting producer community co-operatives especially in the Gaelic areas, and these were known by the Gaelic term '*co-chomainn*'.

Around 1980 it set up a Gaelic committee which called for evidence on the economic, social and cultural situation of the language and commissioned Martin MacDonald, a freelance journalist and broadcaster, to produce a report. This was published in 1982 under the title *Cor na Gàidhlig* – Language, Community and Development, the Gaelic Situation, a report... with recommendations for action.'

These recommendations were the most authoritative and well-researched statement of a policy for Gaelic that had ever been formulated. It was as impressive a report as that produced by the Government's specifically funded Commission for the Welsh Language, whose report, 'A Future for the Welsh Language', had appeared in 1978. Yet the corresponding body in Scotland was a sub-committee of a quango concerned with regional development – and it is important to remember that although the Board had by that time taken on a Gaelic remit, the language was spoken by 33,410 natives and migrants outwith the boundaries of its area of benefit – or 42.1% of Scotland's 1981 total of 79,307 Gaelic speakers. It was tackling a national task without national funding.

The report identified institutional gaps in such fields as education, broadcasting, publishing and the popular arts. But it went further, to identify more fundamental shortcomings in the 'fragmentation of effort and lack of liaison, misconceptions and outdated stereotypes of the nature of the Gaelic community, a tendency to isolate the linguistic aspect from other aspects of community development, and the lack of sophisticated research into communal development.' It called for a new co-ordinating and development organisation for the language, officially recognised and publicly acountable, with a national rather than merely a Highland remit. A costed structure and a developmental programme for such an organisation was detailed and a name was suggested.

A number of further initiatives were subjoined relating to Gaelic and tourism, youth activity projects, further assistance for Gaelic playgroups, an audio-visual unit, Gaelic promotional goods, an annual non-competitive Gaelic cultural festival, Gaelic periodicals, and the implications of *Fèis Bharraigh* as a model for other local Gaelic community festivals. Specific recommendations were made to the HIDB and the Scottish Office, many of which came to be adopted and implemented over the ensuing few years. Thus much of the progress of the official recognition of Gaelic during the '80s can be attributed to this report.

In 1984 the HIDB appointed a Gaelic Development Officer, and initiated a Gaelic development programme under the aegis of its Social Development Officer. It gave practical assistance to *Comhairle nan Sgoiltean Araich* (the Gaelic Playgroups Association) in acquiring staff and headquarters, it funded an organisation for Gaelic learners: *Comann an Luchd-Ionnsachaidh (CLì)*, but most importantly established *Comunn na Gàidhlig (CnaG)* on lines recommended in the *Cor na Gàidhlig* report. These bodies came to share premises together in Inverness but independently of the HIDB and, for much of their earlier existence also, with *An Comunn Gàidhealach,* which continued as an independent voluntary Gaelic cultural organisation. In that *CnaG* was now given an officially recognised remit for the promotion of Gaelic in public life, including education, there was some indeterminacy and friction between these two organisations, the senior of which had been left with a vague cultural role and the National *Mòd*.

Eventually there was a rapprochement between them and a joint statement of their respective complementary rles was issued prior to a joint appointment of a Gaelic Arts Officer (with assistance from the Scottish Arts Council) in 1987.

In June 1985 *CnaG* and *Sabhal Mór Ostaig* convened a representative conference at the Gaelic College entitled 'Towards a National Policy for Gaelic'. All bodies whether voluntary, public service or commercial having an interest and a bearing on Gaelic were invited to send delegates, and the event was addressed by George Younger, Secretary of State. The text of his speech was the nearest thing to an official governmental policy statement which had appeared to date, but it fell far short of the Llanrwst speech of Nicholas Edwards, as Secretary of State for Wales, in 1980 (which had been published as 'The Government's Policy for the Welsh Language'). George Younger gave some tacit official recognition of Gaelic and the role of *CnaG*, and he announced that there would be a specific grant for educational projects. This took effect in the ensuing year and provided a budget of £250,000. Such a fund had been a recommendation of the '*Cor na Gàidhlig*' report. The importance of this fund increased over the years and by the late '80s had quadrupled, approaching an annual total of £1m. Following the conference *CnaG* produced its own report 'Towards a National Policy for Gaelic' in 1986. This outlined the objectives which *CnaG* regarded as essential for safeguarding the future of the language, and developed the initiative of the earlier recommendations for action, some of which had already been implemented.

In 1989, *CnaG* published its 'Gaelic Progress Report' commissioning Martin MacDonald, who had prepared the *Cor na Gàidhlig* study which had reported in 1982. During its first five years, *CnaG* had been active in promoting Gaelic working parties and ten-year development plans in the Gaelic areas, covering the Western Isles, Skye, Mull and Islay, establishing Gaelic youth clubs for primary and secondary aged children in the Western Isles, Skye, Oban and Glasgow, the youth radio project *Guth na h-òige* (Voice of Youth), Gaelic summer youth camps, a Gaelic interpretation project *Ìomhaigh* (Image), convening conferences on television and broadcasting policy, prompting an Inter-Authority Standing Group on Gaelic Education, and establishing a National Gaelic Arts Project, as well as lobbying on various Gaelic issues. Early on it appointed an education officer and three local field officers to promote and carry out these policies.

The report also detailed developments undertaken in the media, and commercial and economic life, drawing special attention to the number of jobs which it estimated at around 40 in the media and 200 in the commercial sector which called for some knowlege of Gaelic. The report emphasised that progress towards this could be hampered by a dearth of Gaelic speakers with the requisite skills resulting from the low base of education supplying them. Attention was drawn to rapidly-increasing demand for Gaelic education and the crisis in provision of resources and training. The report commended *CnaG* for its concentration on pressing issues in broadcasting policy, but drew attention to the potential neglect of other vital areas. It called for an appointment of an officer to stimulate Gaelic-related activities in the economic sector and realise the commercial potential of the language.

A further field in which official support for the language has developed has been within European Community institutions. The Arfé Resolutions of 1981 and 1983 requested national governments to implement rights and facilities for lesser-used languages in education from nursery-school to university, in mass-communications, and in public life and social affairs. It led to the establishment of the European Bureau for Lesser-Used Languages in 1982. This was originally set up in the premises of *Bord na Gaeilge* in Dublin on something of a budgetary shoe-string, but as finances have gradually improved it has acquired premises of its own elsewhere in Dublin. The Arfé Resolutions were followed in 1987 by the Kuijpers Resolution, which called for the principles and proposals of the former resolutions on languages and cultures of regional and ethnic minorities to be fully implemented, and set out a detailed programme for the practical recognition and support of all the EC lesser-used languages on an equitable and common footing.

The EC recognises thirty-four cases of indigenous minority languages in the territories of its twelve member-states. In some cases these are majority languages in other state-territories, and the number also includes cases of minority languages which are represented in more than one member-state. The benefits which Scottish Gaelic have received from this recognition are modest but nevertheless important. Studies of pre-school and primary level education have focused upon each of the thirty-four languages individually, and comparison of practice between education systems has been valuable. Travelling bursaries through a Study Visit Programme have enabled cultural 'multipliers' from the lesser-used languages communities to visit others to study their educational and cultural institutions. In 1987 a Scottish Gael, the Rev. Jack MacArthur, became President of the Bureau, holding office until 1989. The Bureau has convened international seminars on such matters as children's book publication (Stornoway, May 1987), and primary schooling (Riis, Friesland, April 1988).

The Council of Europe has twenty-one member-states including the United Kingdom, and the European Court of Justice at the Hague was established under its aegis. In some respects this acts as a final court of appeal for member states. A few days before the European Parliament's 1981 Arfé Resolution, the Council of Europe adopted a resolution and report on European Regional and Minority Languages: This led to its Standing Conference of Local and Regional Authorities organising a public hearing on the question in May 1984, and setting up a working party to prepare the text of draft charter. This covered education, public services, administrative and legal authorities, media, cultural facilities and activities, economic and social life.

The progress of this charter may be slow as it proceeds from the Standing Conference to the Parliamentary Assembly and the Committee of ministers. If

in the case of procurators-fiscal as in that of sheriffs'
(pp. 82/83) Not until a century later, in the 1984
Montgomery Report (on Scottish Islands Areas
Administration) was there another substantial call for
recognition or support for Gaelic language and culture in any official government report.

The inquiry had before it almost ten years' experience of the Scottish islands areas which had been set
up as part of the 1975 reforms of Scottish local
government. A case had been made for these as areas
of distinctive culture and even language. Small in
population, they were unique at the time as one-tier
'most purpose' authorities discharging both district
and regional powers, which had given the Western
Isles a unique opportunity in implementing its Gaelic
policies. Following its example, four other local
authorities have also formulated bilingual policies
and have constituted Gaelic committees. These are
Highland Region, Skye & Lochalsh District, Ross &
Cromarty District, and most recently Argyll & Bute
District. Although Strathclyde Regional Council has
finally ratified it will be open to signature by member-
states as a binding convention. This would enable
language issues to be brought ultimately to the European Court. Needless to say, the United Kingdom has
tabled reservations, and France has voiced strong
opposition.

Recognition for Gaelic has come some way since
the first call for language-rights over a century ago in
the Report of the Royal Commission (Highlands and
Islands) 1883, the 'Napier Report'. This had criticised
sheriff-substitutes 'ignorant of the habitual language
of the ₊people', and recommended 'the important
qualification of a knowledge of Gaelic.....as desirable

not yet constituted a Gaelic committee as such, it has designated a councillor with responsibility for Gaelic.

The Montgomery Report was defective in its view of the geographical distribution of Gaelic speakers, concluding that 'Gaelic concerns only a small number of authorities largely in one part of Scotland and spanning only parts of some local authority areas' (Ch. 6–11), but as with the Napier Report a century earlier it did call for recognition of Gaelic in local administration. It was similarly limited in identifying the education service as having the principal task in preservation and promotion of Gaelic (Ch. 5–11) It should be said that all public services have responsibilities for language-use and maintenance. To some extent this was implicit in its recommendation that 'Government should take the initiative, consulting with all relevant parties, in working out a broad policy for Gaelic and in allocating responsibilities and resources between the parties, central government, local authorities and other agencies in carrying out the policy.'

With the creation of *CnaG* later in the same year, an officially recognised body had been created which could undertake such a task. In its dealings with the Secretary of State, its objectives were clearly to secure some such officially recognised national policy. In April 1987 the occasion of the Celtic Film Festival at Inverness was to have been the opportunity for the then Secretary of State, Malcolm Rifkind, to have delivered a follow-up speech to George Younger's of 1985 on the government's response to *CnaG's* work and its report, 'Towards a National Gaelic Policy'. The speech was delivered by James Scott, Secretary to the Scottish Education Department, in the absence of the Secretary of State through indisposition. Its tone was positive, it reviewed and approved the recent progress in the Gaelic field, and expressed confidence in the work of *CnaG* but the idea of a National Policy was tacitly rejected. George Younger's earlier promises were re-iterated, '...that if the Gaelic community brought ideas forward, the Government... would respond', seeing *CnaG* as the proper vehicle for their articulation. Commitment was forthcoming for the Specific Grants Scheme, Gaelic-medium education at playgroup and primary levels and at *Sabhal Mór Ostaig*. The speech concluded with a vision of Gaelic as 'not just the language of the past....the language of the future too.'

Such commitment deserves to be more positively signalled at least by legislation defining the status of the language, and some concerted policy involving all levels of administration. The reluctance of the United Kingdom to commit itself by statute on its language-policies may mean that its language legislation gets made for it by European institutions as European countries develop closer political association and common practice.

COMMUNICATION

Cha b'e sneachda 's an reothadh bho thuath,
Cha b'e 'n crannadh geur fuar bho'n ear,
Cha b'e 'n uisge 's an gaillionn bho'n iar,
Ach an galar a bhlian bho'n deas —
Blàth, duilleach, stoc agus freumh
Cànain mo threubh 's mo shluaigh.

Thugainn, thig còmh' rium gu siar
Gus an cluinn sinn ann cànain na Finn!
Thugainn, thig còmh' rium gu siar
Gus an cluinn sinn ann cànan nan Gàidheal!
Murchadh MacPhàrlain: CÀNAN NAN GÀIDHEAL

It's not the snow and the frost from the north,
It's not the sharp cold withering from the east,
It's not the rain and the storm from the west,
But the sickness that blights from the south —
Blossom, foliage, stem and root
Of the tongue of my kin and my folk.

Come away, come with me to the west
Until we hear there the tongue of Fionn's warriors!
Come away, come with me to the west
Until we hear there the language of the Gaels!
Murdo MacFarlane: *THE LANGUAGE OF THE GAELS*

Speaking in a television feature shortly before he died, Murdo MacFarlane, the Melbost bard, said to his interviewers,

'How I envy you people here! You are not faced with my problem. Just imagine if you were going home tonight and you were saying to yourself, 'The language I am speaking will will be dead in sixty years.'....it's so discouraging, but still we sing, and still we make songs in spite of everything!' ('And Still They Sing' BBC2, 10/9/80) MacFarlane's verse has a radical cast to it, at times decrying the mad rush of today's world, militarism, atomic weaponry and nuclear pollution. Here, in one of his latter songs, he laments the shrinking of the Gaelic world to the is-lands of the west – and indites the creeping sickness from the south that blights the flourishing of his Gaelic culture.

If today's Gaeldom is shrivelled and sapped by the sickness from the south, it has nevertheless generated some vigorous development in culture and the arts. The creativity of its modern literature both in prose and verse may never have been higher, despite para-doxically the contracted numbers of its speakers. In recent years there have been many new developments in the Gaelic arts. They have however to contend for attention with the flood-tide of English-language cul-ture delivered by the media into every home of the Gàidhealtachd.

There has been a substantial history of Gaelic broadcasting – almost from the first days of radio in Scotland. The first Gaelic programme, a 15-minute religious address, was transmitted on 2nd December 1923 from Aberdeen, but output was small and spor-adic until after the war. There were some modest increases in the late '40s and early '50s but output had only reached 1½ hours per week by the mid-'50s, running at about 2¾ hours per week by the early '60s, and 3¼ hours by the late '60s. For a year or two thereafter the situation improved further, and at times between 3-5 hours per week were being broadcast. These programmes were carried on the Scottish Home Service only – the precursor of Radio 4 and Radio Scotland. With the introduction of VHF and the reorganisation of services in the late '60s and early '70s, Gaelic programmes were transferred almost in total to VHF in 1974, which made them 'very hard to find' over much of the Hebrides and western Highlands, but improvements gradually occurred and with the establishment of Radio Highland from Inverness in 1976, and more particulary *Radio nan Eilean* from Stornoway in 1979, substantial improvements in output occurred.

These improvements occurred in the wake of the Crawford and Annan Reports into broadcasting. The Crawford Report in 1974 recommended a Gaelic radio output of between 13-18 hours per week, but saw little prospect for improvement for Gaelic television time. The reactions of Gaeldom to this report, and to the invidious comparisons made with its treatment of Welsh, meant that representations to the ensuing Annan Committee were copious and well-argued. The recommendations of the Annan Report in 1977 however contained very little progress for Gaelic and rejected any comparison with Welsh. Its understanding of the geography and demography of Gaeldom was factually inadequate, but during this period there were gradual changes in attitude towards Gaelic broadcasting. It came to be seen not just as another minority interest which people could take up like gardening or did as job like farming, but as a language and culture in its own right within which its speakers might be interested to develop a range of interests, as English speakers do. The idea of a Gaelic broadcasting service catering for all aspects of life through the medium of Gaelic medium at last came came to be appreciated. A typical 'Gaelic programme' might then no longer be a recital of Kennedy-Fraser songs introduced in English, with piano accompaniment.

With the promotion of Neil Fraser, from heading the Gaelic Department to running BBC Scotland, Gaelic broadcasting was reorganised in 1985 under the banner of *Radio nan Gàidheal* providing nationwide output from Glasgow, Highland coverage from Inverness, Hebridean and west-coast transmission from Stornoway. About 28 hours were being provided by the late '80s. The increased airtime led to a greater diversification of programmes and some example of almost every genre of broadcasting in Gaelic was being developed – including Gaelic commentary on the international match from Wembley. The intention was to expand *Radio nan Gàidheal* into a fulltime Gaelic channnel on the lines of BBC Radio Cymru. Disappointment with the licence fee in the following year ruled this out – but the intention remains, albeit for the present on the back burner.

Two avenues of pressure are apparent in the improvements secured in Gaelic broadcasting. There has always been a 'numbers argument' based on proportions of Gaelic-speakers in local, regional and national populations. For example, it can be shown that about 20% of the Highlands and Islands population is Gaelic-speaking – and on this argument might claim one-fifth of airtime on BBC for their own linguistic and cultural needs. There are six BBC channels serving this area: Radios 1 to 5, plus BBC Radio Scotland and its local opt-outs. Gaelic-speakers might equitably claim one of the channels – or since they are virtually all bilingual and benefit from English-language broadcasting, at least half a channel for their own service. That would produce between 70-140 hours per week. On this argument also, a national service of between 6-11 hours could be claimed in order to serve the 1.64% of Scotland's population which is Gaelic speaking. The broadcasting authorities have never responded to this argument, but current nationally-networked radio provision does not fall far short of it. Regionally however, in the Highlands and Hebrides provision is still well below a level proportional to the Gaelic population.

The BBC was swift to react to street demonstrations for more airtime for Gaelic in 1974/75. These were organised first by the Glasgow branch of the recently-formed Gaelic students' organisation, *COGA (Comhairle Oileanaich Ghàidhealach Alba)*. Their march on Broadcasting House Glasgow in December 1974 was a modest affair of about thirty people. It was first ignored by the BBC, but gleefully featured on STV news. This resulted in a further demonstration in January 1975, involving about 200 people, with pipes and banners, including students from other universities, and had even put their academics and the Gaelic establishment on the spot in joining them. Improvements in the BBC Gaelic service seemed rapidly to follow, including the constitution of a Gaelic Advisory

Committee in 1976. A decade later the demonstration tactic was repeated – this time with a sit-in at Scottish Television's headquarters at Cowcaddens.

The broadcasting authorities have also responded to more conventional approaches. *An Comunn Gàidhealach* and *Comunn na Gàidhlig* have both undertaken studies of the broadcasting situation, and have produced well-researched reports. The authoritative report commissioned by *An Comunn Gàidhealach*, following the Government's 1978 White Paper on Broadcasting, provided an excellent factual account of the history of Gaelic broadcasting to date, but unfortunately it was never made public. Its nuggets of information stemming from an intimate inside knowledge may thus never contribute to wider enlightenment. Its authoritative comparisons with other minority language broadcasting services, detailed critique of current programming, and reasoned recommendations were thus never enabled to inform contemporary debate, but it is remarkable how readily they were in fact taken up in broadcasting practice in the ensuing period.

CnaG a decade later has taken the trouble, in its campaigns to secure improved broadcasting facilities for Gaelic, to convene representative conferences in various localities and has commissioned professional research published its conclusions in 1989 with reports on both radio and television broadcasting. It is quite clear today that the broadcasting media have been identified as a crucial field affecting the survival of the language. The cultural influence of powerful communications media – especially upon the young – has operated as a strongly anglicising factor. With the advent of television in the Gaelic areas from the mid-

'60s, it came to be realised by representative Gaelic
organisations, by the community and its elected
authorities, and finally by broadcasting authorities
themselves that an adequate Gaelic broadcasting service in both media would be crucial for the language's
survival.

The first Gaelic television programmes were sta-
gey, outside broadcasts of platform concerts from the
National *Mòd*, not in those days without their technical hitches. The first was in 1952 and was compèred
'in the poor English' by *An Comunn's* general secretary, Neil Shaw. As with the then Welsh programmes they were networked throughout the
system. The first truly Gaelic feature was a television
play, *Ceann Cropaig* (Crappit Heid) by Finlay Mac-
Leod, made in monochrome and broadcast in the
early '70s. The recording now seems to have been
wiped. In the early '70s, the BBC's Gaelic output
comprised a weekly current affairs programme *Bonn
Còmhraidh* (Talking Point) and a light entertainment
and music programme *'Se Ur Beatha* (You're Welcome), both of approximately half-an-hour and running for about nine week series in the autumn and
winter seasons. In 1972/3 for one season repeats of *'Se
Ur Beatha* were networked throughout the U.K. The
situation remained much the same throughout the
'70s, with a norm less than 10 hours per year of Gaelic
programming. For the best part of a year following
the resignation of its Gaelic television producer in
September 1978, there was none. This resignation by
Neil Fraser was the third from this post in ten years.

Meanwhile, ITV was stealing a march on BBC.
With the opening of the Eitshal transmitter in Lewis
in 1976, Grampian Television produced a lively series

of Saturday morning children's programmes in Gaelic, which became popular with non-Gaelic viewers. The Annan Report regarded Grampian as the appropriate source of ITV Gaelic programming (despite the fact that half the Gaelic population lived in the STV area), and Grampian rose to this challenge producing a number of Gaelic music programmes, an expanded weekly Gaelic current affairs magazine throughout the year, a number of special features in Gaelic on the arts, and maintaining its lead in children's television. With some reorganisation of its services in 1985, BBC made its priority children's programming, and ran daily 10-minute children's programmes from then on. The traditional week of Mòd coverage was relinquished to ITV. A current affairs series with a half-hour slot on BBC2, *Prosbaig* (Spyglass) focused on investigative journalism, at times pulling off 'scoops' to be picked up in the next morning's papers.

A series for the 15-25 age-group was produced in the mid-'80s. Thus, by 1989 the BBC's annual Gaelic output was about 40 hours of children's programming, and 20 hours for adults, boosted by a week in which about six hours of Gaelic programming (*Toradh na Gàidhlig* – Produce of Gaelic) was screened – mainly at peak times.

This last venture gave some indication of the minimum that should be provided weekly on television, and does not seem to have resulted in adverse audience reaction. The BBC's frequently cited fear of offending its non-Gaelic audience has probably been more of an excuse than a reason for inaction. The broadcasting authorities have never expressed similar fears in screening foreign-language films. These can be subtitled or dubbed, as could Gaelic programmes. The technology already exists for subtitling on Cee-fax – as is already done for deaf viewers. A national public opinion survey undertaken by System Three in 1989 for *CnaG* elicited a 67% support for a Gaelic television channel, with 77% in favour of special provision for Gaelic viewers, and 76% in favour of the current £2.6m levy on Scottish ITV companies for Welsh-language television going to Gaelic instead.

This might be compared with a similar national survey undertaken by my own research unit for *An Comunn Gàidhealach* in 1981 which elicited 39% (49% eliminating 'don't knows), supporting more or much more broadcasting time for Gaelic, compared with 41% for none or less than at present. 82% of respondents reported having viewed or heard Gaelic broadcasts. Indeed some non-Gaelic respondents commented favourably on the recent *Tormod air Telly* (Norman on Telly) series featuring the Gaelic comedian, Norman MacLean.

The Peacock Report of 1986 had compared Welsh and Gaelic-language broadcasting facilties, and *CnaG* was quick to take the initiative in promoting representative conferences, producing authoritative reports and commissioning a survey of public opinion following the Commons statement by the Home Office Minister for Broadcasting (Timothy Renton), and aimed at the debate of the Scottish Grand Committee on the 1988 Broadcasting White Paper. It is a sign of progress that there is now a representative Gaelic body which anticipates events rather than merely reacting to them.

In other fields of communications, Gaeldom has shown the capacity to develop with the times. Until it became an early victim of local government and Arts Council economies a Gaelic theatre company, *Fir Chlis* (Northern Lights) based in the Western Isles toured annually between 1978 and 1982. The *7.84 Company* has subsequently toured with bilingual productions – but the Arts Council also recently axed its grant. Amateur Gaelic drama has become a vigorous and popular scene over the past decade, and deserves a complementary professional theatre. In 1989 *An Comunn Gàidhealach* promoted a successful Gaelic Youth Drama Festival. A Gaelic community film unit *Cinema Sgire* (District Cinema) – another victim of the cuts in 1981 – developed into *Sùil* (Eye) and the Celtic Film Festival with headquarters in Inverness, running annual festivals in the six Celtic countries. A professional Gaelic film and video unit *Fradharc Ur* (New Vision) set up in Lewis in 1987, and is training young Gaels in film and video production. Gaelic video and television production companies have subsequently been formed, such as *Bocsa Beò* and *Abu Tele*.

In December 1989 the Government announced an 8m Gaelic Television Broadcasting Fund which would treble the amount of Gaelic television broadcasting to some 200 hours annually. This was the culmination of some years' intensive lobbying by *CnaG* (and some decades' efforts of other individuals and organisations). It was warmly welcomed by representative Gaelic organisations and opposition parties, and especially by organisations with involvement in the media such as Abu Tele and Media nan Eilean. There ensued considerable public debate, especially in the press as to how the money should be spent. The fund would be administered by the Independent

Television Commission and the programming would be carried on the Channel Three network by Grampian and Scottish Television (and their franchise successors) but BBC channels in Scotland might also participate. In announcing this development at a St Andrew's House press conference, Malcolm Rifkind said, 'It will provide the Gaelic community with an adequate broadcasting service for the first time, and re-affirm the Government's commitment to Gaelic language and culture....It therefore has a very special role, relevant...to Scottish culture and to the wider culture of these islands as a whole.' This announcement was clearly a breakthrough not only in the development of the Gaelic media, but also in the Government's recognition of the importance of Gaelic as one of the principal indigenous languages of the United Kingdom.

The recording industry has also been a field which has responded well to opportunities in Gaelic culture. In the 78 era, poor wireless reception in the Gaelic areas, and a lively expatriate culture led to 'fortunes being made', according to a *Gairm* article (No. 14, Winter 1955), marking the appearance of the *Gaelfonn* label. By the 1950s the field had almost entirely been left to the Beltona company. The advent of the long-player opened a new era for Gaelic recordings, to be followed by developments in cassette tape. The folk-groups competition introduced at the 1972 National *Mòd* encouraged the formation of new Gaelic pop/folk groups, in the wake of *Na h-Oganaich*, the first winners. Since then quite a number of such popular Gaelic combinations have come and gone. The rock group *Run-Rig* was an early development and has shown staying power, matched more recently

by Capercaillie. In 1984, the National Mòd introduced *Ceòl is Cleas* (Music and Action): a new music
and drama group competition for teenagers, and
similar developments have followed at local *Mòds*.

In publishing there is a need for a regular all-
Gaelic newspaper, and Gairm, founded in 1952, is
still the only regular all-Gaelic magazine. However,
the *Stornoway Gazette, West Highland Free Press, Oban
Times*, and the Saturday edition of *The Scotsman* all
carry regular Gaelic features. There has been a remarkable up-turn in Gaelic book publication since
1970 – greater than at any time since the first printed
Gaelic book appeared in 1567. Government finance
and educational developments have both contributed
greatly to this expansion.

The Gaelic Books Council was established under
the aegis of the Glasgow University Celtic Department in 1968, and since then it has disbursed over
£200,000 in publication grants. With Scottish Arts
Council funding it has also commissioned, edited,
publicised, catalogued and retailed Gaelic books.
With such assistance, Gairm Publications (whose first
title appeared in 1958) greatly increased its output in
the 1970s, and still continues vigorously, whilst Club
Leabhar, the Highland Bookclub, produced about
twenty titles during this period. Despite an interesting
booklist, it foundered around 1980, and its last title
appeared in 1984. Its place in Gaelic publishing was
more than taken over by Acair, established in Stornoway in 1977. Acair has been particularly active in
educational publishing, with a particularly impressive
children's book-list.

In fact the greatest expansion in Gaelic publishing
has been in this area, with about a quarter of the

Gaelic Book Council's grants going to children's books. The Scottish Education Department Specific Grants Scheme has considerably boosted this sector since 1986, with fifty Gaelic titles for children and young people appearing in 1989. Developments in other fields have been slower, affected by the dearth of full-time Gaelic writers, but poetry is well represented, together with interesting work in fiction, autobiography and social history. About thirty new titles appear annually, with about three-hundred currently in print. Smaller publishers include Glasgow University Celtic Department, Crùisgean, An Comunn Gàidhealach, Leabhraichean Beaga and Clò Chailleann. These developments have been recognised at Frankfurt Book Fair, where there is a section for 'Books in Gaelic', and have gone hand-in-hand with the considerable increases in Gaelic literacy over the past thirty years.

It will be appropriate therefore next to consider the progress in Gaelic education which has enabled this to happen. But in conclusion it can be noted that in reaction to *'an galar a bhlian bho'n deas'* (– 'the sickness that blights from the south'), Gaelic culture has developed some vigorous cultural antibodies. Given support from within the community, and a fair share of society's resources, these could yet restore the language to full health.

EDUCATION

'*An t-ionnsachadh òg – an t-ionnsachadh bòidheach*' (*seanfhacal Gàidhlig*).
'Learning young – learning handsome' (Gaelic proverb.)

The fifteen years up to 1990 has been a period of accelerating development for Gaelic education. One of the first initiatives of *Comhairle nan Eilean* in 1975 was to introduce a Bilingual Education Project at primary level. This got under way in 1976 with government support, and the first phase lasting until 1978 involved twenty of the authority's fifty-nine primary schools. Its second phase from 1976-81 consolidated experience and applied its methods and materials in a further fourteen schools. Thereafter the policy was extended to all the authority's primary schools and their pupils.

In extending this policy to the secondary level in 1979, the *Comhairle*'s resolve faltered and the matter was moved back for further consideration. When it was eventually adopted later that year there had been a change of government and the incoming Conservative administration was reluctant to fund a similar bilingual project at the secondary stage. Instead, the Scottish Education Department commissioned an independent study from Stirling University Department of Education to evaluate the success of the primary project. This was intended as a two-year study and a precondition for the funding of a secondary project. It eventually commenced in 1984 and was completed in 1986. The report was released in April 1987.

The Western Isles project was very much the front runner in Gaelic educational developments at this time, although Highland Region was already providing tuition in Gaelic as a second language in many of its primary schools, often as the result of parental pressure and local working parties stimulated by *An Comunn*'s education officer, Colin Spencer. Similar schemes had been set up in Mull and Argyll, and for many years Gaelic had been taught in Tiree. Following the Western Isles example, Highland Region was prompted to sound out parental views in Skye, and a bilingual scheme commenced in the northern half of Skye in 1978. By 1985 this had been extended to all Skye schools.

The Western Isles Evaluative Study broadly confirmed the value and effectiveness of the Western Isles Bilingual Education Project in primary education, and found that the project had been highly effective in being accepted and implemented by teachers, and bilingual teaching was well established across the curriculum.

The language development of bilingual children had benefited, and there was no evidence of any negative linguistic effects. There was considerable implementation of project ideas by all schools in the sample. The particular interests of the project were thoroughly integrated with the curriculum as a whole. Environmental studies and Gaelic language-arts were the most marked successes. The transformation to a more child-centred method of teaching, and significant parental and community involvement were of more limited success. The recruitment of local Gaelic-speaking teachers was the cornerstone on which the policy relied. The conclusions did identify certain policy gaps, in particular, resource limitations and the need for clearer policy on teaching Gaelic to English-speaking children, without which the existing model of bilingual education would become relevant to fewer and fewer schools.

The Project had focused on native Gaelic-speaking children, attempting to provide a systematic structure to develop all the capabilities of bilingual children, developing integrated, experiential, child-centred methods of learning and teaching together with materials appropriate to a Gaelic-English bilingual curriculum of direct relevance to island children. The report noted that there was clearly an implicit aim of language-maintenance – but this was never explicitly stated. A further underlying purpose was that the Western Isles education authority considered that for Gaelic-speaking children a bilingual curriculum was necessary in order to achieve national primary educational policy.

The study was concerned with home and school links, since the original project had emphasised the involvement of parents and community in children's education. It found ready support for the Project's objectives and methods, and satisfaction also regarding the development of Gaelic literacy, which had often not featured in parents' own education. This extended to regret that secondary schooling did not continue the bilingual curriculum. The general absence in Scotland of a tradition of sustained parental and community involvement in the schools meant that the Bilingual Education Project had broken new ground in proposing it, although such involvement had not been very widely achieved.

The evaluative study concluded that the objectives of the Bilingual Education Project had in general been achieved in very full measure, and its policies were clearly desirable. The research team did observe that this had in very large measure been possible owing to the recruitment of local bilingual teachers who were able to develop a bilingual curriculum – even although there had been no specific bilingual element in their own professional education.

The researchers drew attention to the need to ensure the supply of appropriately and bilingually trained teachers from the colleges of education and their appointment to bilingual posts. The report called strongly for consistent provision for bilingual teacher training. It also drew especial attention to the needs of Gaelic learners in Western Isles primary schools – and to the need to provide effective Gaelic second-language teaching of non-Gaelic-speaking pupils in order to ensure the continuation of effective bilingual education. This is urgent if Gaelic is to have a significant place as a teaching medium in Western Isles schools. Visiting teachers should also be system-

atically involved in bilingual education. So far as fully
bilingual school entrants are concerned, existing policy is only just adequate to ensure and maintain their
Gaelic language proficiency. Parents also should be
more fully involved with policy developments in their
children's schools.

Parent power (in the wake of the Government's
'Parents' Charter') was by this time playing an import-
ant part in developments in Gaelic education. Following the Gaelic roadsigns campaign, *Strì* involved itself
in pressure for better radio and television facilities for
Gaelic, but its leading personality, Fionnlaigh Mac-
Leòid quickly involved himself in what was at first a
one-man campaign to promote Gaelic playgroups.
This very rapidly attracted support and in 1982 was
founded *Comhairle nan Sgoiltean Araich* (Council of
Nursery Schools) co-ordinating four *'cròileagain'*
(Gaelic playgroups). These became established both
in urban contexts amongst migrant Gaels and in *Gàidhealtachd* locations as an essential aspect of language-
maintenance even in the Gaelic communities themselves, and by 1990 totalled seventy-six, catering for
1,200 children. In 1984 HIDB funding enabled headquarters to be established in Inverness with permanent staff, which greatly assisted the growth of the
movement. Parent and toddler groups (*'Buidhnean
Pàrant is Pàiste'*) were founded, growing from seven in
that year to twenty in 1989.

The first four *cròileagain* led to demand for continuing Gaelic-medium education at primary level, and
in 1985 Gaelic-medium primary units came into
being in Glasgow and Inverness, shortly followed by
Portree (Skye) and Breasclete (Lewis). This was a
historic watershed in Gaelic education. For the first

time the language was being used as the principal teaching medium for the whole of the primary stage. It was happening simultaneously in urban, Highland and Island contexts – and it was parent-led. The role of the playgroups movement in forcing the pace was apparent.

During the next five years the number of Gaelic-medium units trebled, totalling sixteen by the 1989/90 session. There should have been twenty but for expansion in Highland and Strathclyde Regions being impeded by teacher shortage. By this time, Gaelic had entered the school curriculum in three ways: as a specific subject or second language, as a teaching medium bilingually with English, and as a principal teaching medium. In the 1987/88 session (the latest for which figures are currently available) Gaelic was entering into the education, in one or other of these ways, of 10,159 pupils throughout Scotland. At the primary stage there were ninety-seven schools within which it was taught as a subject or second language to 4,219 pupils, bilingually (together with English) as a teaching medium in seventy-four schools to 3,140 pupils, and as a principal teaching medium in four schools to sixty-eight pupils. The 1987/88 statistics can confidently be expected to show substantial increases.

In the 1987/88 session Gaelic was taught as a subject in fourty-one secondary schools to 2,074 pupils. In the Western Isles a pilot project had been developing Gaelic as a teaching medium in two secondary schools between 1983-85, and in 1988 as the first Gaelic-medium cohort proceeded into the secondary stage from Sir John Maxwell Primary School in Glasgow, a Gaelic-medium stream commenced at Hill

Park Secondary. (Current figures for Gaelic in secondary education were likewise not available at the time of writing.) One of the hindrances for Gaelic at the secondary stage is its status vis-à-vis French.

In Highland and Island schools where both languages are taught, a decision is frequently forced upon pupils to drop one in the run-up to leaving examinations. This is generally Gaelic, as French is extolled for its career potential, with developing EC relationships held out as promising job prospects. Yet it is most probably the case that in present-day Scotland there are at least as many jobs requiring ability in Gaelic as French – especially in the media. The national opinion poll commissioned by *An Comunn* in 1981 had found that 70% of its national population sample (or 82% eliminating 'don't knows') agreed that children in any part of Scotland should be able to learn Gaelic at school if they or their parents wanted it. This was the highest level of public support for any of its questions on Gaelic policies. (See Appendix.) If at all representative of public opinion, this view deserves to be reflected in the school curriculum – at least to enable Gaelic wherever it is taught to be studied with or without French as a matter of free choice.

The situation was not assisted by governmental policy as communicated by SED Circular 1178 in January 1989. This stipulated that a modern European foreign language was to be studied by all pupils throughout the four years of compulsory secondary schooling. The tacit definition of these languages as consisting of French, German, Italian, Spanish and Russian includes a language other than an EC official language and excludes five others in contrast to the

English National Curriculum. The position of Gaelic together with Asian and Classical languages was thus jeopardised, as their status was tacitly relegated to that of additional languages offered from the first two secondary years. Following representations by education authorities, *CnaG* and others, the situation was further revised by SED Circular 2/1990 to enable Gaelic, Asian and Classical languages to be taught as additional languages also from years Secondary Three and Four.

Where pupils and parents wished, Gaelic or any other language may be taken as the sole language other than English in S3 and S4 (after taking a modern foreign language in S1 and S2). Circular 1178 is thus still under revision, but the current situation still places Gaelic together with Asian and Classical languages at a disadvantage in a system essentially thirled to a sole language of study in the secondary stage. Neither is the status of Gaelic assisted by its designation as an 'enrichment' rather than a 'core subject' by the Scottish Consultative Council on the Curriculum in its 'Guidelines on the Curriculum in the Secondary School'. This is in contrast to the situation in Wales, where Welsh is defined as a core subject in the National Curriculum (and as is Irish in Irish-medium schools in Northern Ireland). It would be a most welcome development for Gaelic if it enjoyed similar status, with pupils being able to choose to take any one or two languages on offer in their schools throughout the secondary stage.

There has been a growing demand over this period for Gaelic tuition in adult education. A survey by *CLi*, the Gaelic Learners' Association, in 1986 indicated ninety-eight evening classes, nine crash-courses, six weekend courses and seven summer-schools teaching the language throughout Scotland. It would be difficult to estimate the student numbers involved. An average of twelve students (generally regarded as the economic minimum) per course would produce a notional total of 1440. In 1979 the BBC produced a television Gaelic learners' course *Can Seo* (Say This) which became the most popular language course ever shown on television in Scotland, and was twice repeated. A national network of *Can Seo* groups came into being, and it was a great pity that this impetus was not maintained with a follow-up series and a regular magazine programme for Gaelic learners. ITV ran a learners' series in a brief early evening slot, *Beagan Gàidhlig* (A Little Gaelic) for a short while thereafter.

The Gaelic College, *Sabhal Mór Ostaig*, started in 1972/73 as a centre for occasional and summer courses in Gaelic. These have continued following the inception of fulltime HND and HNC courses in business and *Gàidhealtachd* studies in 1983, business studies with information technology in 1987, and business studies with office technology in 1989, all taught through the medium of Gaelic. In 1987 a lecturer was appointed to develop an adult learners' course in Gaelic, concurrently with the initiation of a computer-assisted database project on terminology. An audio beginners' course had been developed at Napier College, Edinburgh in the early '70s, and at Telford College distance learning 'Flexi-Study' courses were started in 1983. These have provided a useful follow-on from the National Extension College (Cambridge) SCE O-Grade course, *Gàidhlig Bheò* (Living Gaelic), which had been available since 1976. The

Telford courses take students up to Highers. Lews Castle College, Stornoway is currently preparing an Open Learning course. Modules for Gaelic as a generic modern language have also been developed and from 1989 have been offered for Scottish Vocational Education Council (SCOTVEC) National Certificate courses. Highland Region Community Education broke new ground in 1988 with a literacy course for native Gaelic speakers – a field which has received little attention apart from a short radio series on Radio Highland in the late '70s. There have also been Gaelic courses for HIDB staff, parents and teachers, and other public services personnel.

The level of demand for the language during this period can be gauged by the sales of the late Roderick MacKinnon's *Teach Yourself Gaelic*, which has gone through eighteen impressions since its first appearance in 1971. There have been reprints of other learners' texts, and numbers of new courses and learners' aids and materials to match. For example, *Dearc* Software in Inverness produces Gaelic learners' computer material.

Schools broadcasting in Gaelic started early in 1970. This was originally carried on northwest transmitters only, and was in fact paid for by the then Ross-shire and Inverness-shire education authorities. In 1975 this service was taken over and funded by the BBC, and a Gaelic Schools producer was appointed. In 1980 a learners' course, *Tòiseach Tòiseachaidh* (Beginning at the Beginning) was broadcast, aimed at top primary and secondary levels – but which could also cater for adults.

A gap in this field is a post-Highers course in Gaelic language and Gaelic Studies. The *Sabhal Mór Ostaig courses are in business studies as such, albeit with a Gàid-healtachd* studies module. There have been Gaelic bilingual secretaries' courses at Lews Castle College, and from 1989 Gaelic has been offered on SCOT-VEC courses. But these are all fulltime courses, as are the Celtic degree courses at Aberdeen, Edinburgh and Glasgow Universities. There is nothing on the lines of Open University courses in Gaelic language, literature or culture, and such developments would be very worthwhile. The numbers involved in Gaelic adult education should be some indication of potential.

The interest in Gaelic amongst adults, and its place as a school subject are by themselves unlikely to bring about any real development of fluency, or extension of the effective speech-community. Unless language-familiarisation has occurred by age eight, the language is unlikely to be salient in a person's inner speech, and unless there has been effective acquisition by about the end of the primary stage, there is unlikely to be a native ease of use. Fluency can be developed later, but it is hard to win, and it can only then be as a second language. To acquire a language as a child takes about 2,500 hours of active exposure and learning – and this needs to commence directly the child engages in social speech – hence the importance of Gaelic-medium playgroups and primary education. Outwith the native community, only the children in the *cròileagain* and Gaelic-medium units can be realistically regarded as the potential fluent speakers of Gaelic. In SED Circular 1178 the Secretary of State has recognised that in Scotland Gaelic has pioneered the introduction of languages other than English at the primary stage, as a teaching medium, bilingually and as a second language. With the policy to introduce other languages into the primary stage, the place of Gaelic has been officially affirmed. The successes of Gaelic primary education should be a valuable resource and experience for other languages as well.

In 1989/90 Gaelic playgroups presently provide opportunities for 1,200 children. Bilingual primary schooling in the Gaelic communities presently caters for over 3,000 children. Numbers in Gaelic-medium units are currently approching a thousand. John Angus MacKay, Director of *CnaG*, has suggested in a letter (13.6.89), which was made public, to Michael Forsyth, Minister for Education and Health, a target of 2,000 children by the year 2000 receiving Gaelic-medium education by which 'the future of Gaelic will be ensured'. Whether this in itself could ensure the viability of the speech-community is debatable. Unless such children are able to use their Gaelic in viable communities and in a effective range of domains in everyday social life, and to meet and marry Gaelic-speaking partners, with whom they will be motivated to bring up Gaelic-speaking families, education will have done little other than enhance personal accomplishments.

Consideration may now usefully turn to what research has been undertaken on such issues, and what implications it has for the continuation of the language and the viability of the speech community.

PART 3:
PROSPECTS

VIABILITY – THE
RESULTS OF RESEARCH

The studies published by the Committee on Bilingualism of the Scottish Council for Research in Education had a very gradual efffect in changing the educational experience of Gaelic-speaking children. Following these there was a study involving a Gaelic version of the WISC test (Morrison, 1961), and Finlay MacLeod's doctoral study of cognitive performance of bilingual children in Lewis (1969). Both were unpublished academic theses and deserved wider dissemination. Apart from these educational studies, there have been a number of sociological or ethnographic studies of Gaelic communities. Few of these have focused on language as such, and I have attempted over the years to supplement these with a number of studies of the sociology of the language and its speakers.

In this chapter therefore, I wish to summarise the principal findings of these various research studies undertaken within the Gaelic speech-community concerned with language-behaviour and attitudes, and with the use and maintenance of Gaelic.

In any account of how Gaelic survived its neglect in education, Finlay MacLeod's study of cognitive performance amongst bilingual schoolchildren provides an excellent follow-on to Christina Smith's earlier study twenty years previously. Whilst much of his thesis (unpublished but available from Aberdeen University Library) may be at too technical a level for the average reader, his conclusions are clear enough for all. Although working in schools where there was a disposition towards English anyway, he found that children were performing mental operations at a lower level in Gaelic than in English. Their spoken Gaelic was restricted in idiom and vocabulary, whereas their English was more greatly elaborated. He also claimed that when the children spoke Gaelic they tended to use visual modes of thought, but when they used English their thought-processes became abstract and utilised verbal reasoning to a greater extent.

When using Gaelic a child preferred a lower or an easier level of performance, and when using English, a more advanced level was preferred. Children learned to read and write English effectively at school but the formal school situation did not enable them to practise it for themselves: school meant patiently listening and answering the set questions, and it was not a situation where children learned to think for themselves. The children used their English neither as an 'inter-personal' medium nor as an 'intra-personal inner speech' with which to build up strategies and hypotheses for themselves. Hence when brought into contact with strangers or new tasks requiring rapid and flexible use of language, the children were often diffident, defensive and performed poorly.

So far as development of their Gaelic was concerned, the home and the church both had their limitations. In the home, listening was stressed rather than speaking. In the church no provision was made for youth activities. (The Free Presbyterian Church especially opposes youth clubs, drama groups and the like.) Children were not socialised into leadership either by the home or the school (and only in a limited way by the church). MacLeod concluded his study with recommendations for schools in which cognitive development could be promoted both in Gaelic and in English and in which a truly bilingual and bicultural education occurred: each language being allotted a field in which the children could develop confidence and originality and become aware and critical of forces in their environment (for their home, educational and religious culture in the Gaelic community promoted unquestioned acceptance of authority).

Home and religious life have remained strongly Gaelic in Western Isles communities and these powerful associations go a long way to explain the perpetuation of Gaelic in the community, but both are now weakening. MacLeod wondered what the present position would have been had the language of the school have become Gaelic and the language of the church English. In the twenty-odd years since his study, the language of the church has in fact been changing. English services and prayer meetings have been increasing, and one Free Presbyterian minister galvanised a minority languages seminar in Stornoway in

1987 with the news that God Himself was losing confidence in the future of Gaelic, judging by the language of those He was calling to the ministry.

Finlay MacLeod has himself over the past twenty years played a key role in developing the bilingual and bicultural education he called for in 1969, in leaving his university post and returning to Lewis as Gaelic and Primary Schools Adviser, and as the author of innovative plays and childrens books, an authoritative and very readable report on the Gaelic arts and much else.

An earlier scholarly study of a Gaelic community was made by Frank Vallee in Barra in the early '50s. It still has value today in considering the survival of Gaelic sociologically. Vallee reported on the impressive island-wide solidarity of the Barra people — shown particularly in visitations, celebrations and at funerals and that Gaelic and its associated lore and culture provided key symbols for the self-identity of this community. Despite culture-contact with mass-society within an almost totally bilingual community, Gaelic was strongly maintained as one of the means whereby a small community was enabled to be aware of itself as a distinguishable whole in cultural and social terms.

Vallee drew attention to three types of attitude towards Gaelic: (1) that of the 'Gaelic Scholar', immersed in the traditions and literature, self-consciously Gaelic and assertive of standards of purity ; (2) that of the 'Pragmatist' for whom Gaelic and English are equally available and their cultures equally to be enjoyed; (3) a non-Gaelic attitude, rejecting Gaelic culture and identifying with 'mainlandish' ways (then very much a minority position in Barra). 'Socio-

logically,' writes Vallee, '...there is a greater tendency
to use English on the part of individuals of higher
status...in choice situations,' and similarly in the use of
English in business, correspondence and official life.
The 'Gaelic Scholars' included both teachers and individuals of low social status. Nevertheless the 'scholars'
might enjoy considerable social esteem. Even for the
'pragmatist', Gaelic was the language of community
and family solidarity, as well as the tongue in which
he could express the force of his feelings. For everyone, the expressive aspects of local culture are conveyed in Gaelic through songs, anecdotes, etc., at
frequent island ceilidhs.

Since the early '50s the rocket range had been
established in Uist, and its presence had resulted in
permanent settlement of military families. It would
be interesting to assess to what extent Gaelic has
maintained itself there in a very comparable situation
to Barra. It is remarkable just how strongly Gaelic
retains its hold in the affections of its speakers in the
settings of home, church and community. And it is
equally remarkable how Gaelic has been displaced
amongst Gaelic speakers themselves for those aspects
of life which involve business transactions and any
degree of officialdom: the aspects which sociologists
call the transactional and instrumental. For example,
Gaelic speakers will count out change and give the
date in English even in a Gaelic context – so pervasive
have the effects of English-language schooling been
on Gaelic speech-acts. Public meetings are typically in
English – even advertisements of Gaelic events. So
completely has English dominated education, that
until quite recently no-one saw the absurdity of
Gaelic-speaking academics lecturing Gaelic-speaking

students on Gaelic in English.

Joshua Fishman, Professor of Sociology of Language at Yeshiva University, New York, and a leading international scholar in this field, has pointed out that when one language begins to displace another, it is not merely that the receding language comes to be spoken by fewer people, but more significantly its speakers are reduced to those who are less typical of society as a whole. This has been charted very clearly in a Gaelic context by Nancy Dorian in her study of East Sutherlandshire Gaelic in the east-coast village of Embo in the '60s and '70s: 'Language Death', and in a smaller-scale study of Dervaig in Mull. Such perspectives would suppose that Gaelic today is maintained in fringe areas by an independent crofting working class.

Within this community Gaelic tends to be more associated with the old than the young. Its surviving monoglot speakers in the '60s and '70s were typically elderly women. Those who deliberately champion the language within the community came to be the village bards and Gaelic scholars, whilst Gaelic writers and revivalists tended to be those who had left the Gaelic areas to take up professions, particularly the intellectual callings and are in various ways alienated from their origins.

Fishman has drawn attention to what he calls 'third generational return', in which young American Jews sought to relearn the Yiddish their parents and grandparents had forsaken. Something similar can be seen today in the revival of interest amongst people of Gaelic and partly-Gaelic descent. Their parents and grandparents kept Gaelic from them lest it be the handicap they had felt it to be to themselves. Their

descendants now seek to acquire it as adults and –
through playgroups and Gaelic-medium education –
vicariously in their children.

Fishman has also drawn attention to three aspects
of people's attitudes and behaviour regarding language in culture-contact situations. Firstly, there may
be a consciousness of the mother-tongue as an institution distinct from other aspects of the culture. Secondly, there may be a body of commonly shared
knowledge concerning the history of the language
and its different varieties in use. Lastly, there may be
an awareness of the language as a symbol of the
group-life of the community: 'language-loyalty'. For
many Gaelic-speakers there is not a great deal of
awareness of Gaelic as a distinctive institution of social
life. They speak Gaelic – that is natural, and that is
how they communicate – as with Vallee's 'prag-
matists'. English education has consistently attempted
to instil a love of English for its own sake – but until
very recently there has not been a similar official
educational aim for Gaelic. Knowledge and history of
the language, its literature and variants has been
restricted to very few amongst the Gaelic community
– Vallee's 'Gaelic scholars' – and to some extent the
bards, ministers and teachers, and cultivated best
amongst the academics and intellectuals but these
have been located essentially outwith the community.

Perception of the language as a symbol of community in private life and face-to-face communication
was reported by Vallee, and in this has essentially
resided the strength of Gaelic language- maintenance, lacking as it has the kind of official support
forthcoming in Ireland and even Wales.

I have sought to explore further these ideas of Fishman, Vallee and others in various studies of contemporary Gaelic communities. These have principally been: a study of language in education and social life in the Isle of Harris between 1972-74; a study of language and cultural transmission in four Gaelic communities (Southern Harris and Barra in the Western Isles, and the Inverness and St. Ann's areas in Cape Breton Island, Nova Scotia) between 1976-78; a national opinion survey on Gaelic-related issues (including island samples in Skye, Uist and Barra) in 1980-81; and a study of language-maintenance and speech-community viabilty undertaken in Skye and the Western Isles as a whole between 1985-88. The first two studies were assisted by grants from the then Social Science Research Council, the opinion survey was commissioned by *An Comunn Gàidhealach* and funded by the Scottish Education Department, the last study was funded by the Economic and Social Research Council and a smaller grant from Highland Regional Council. In all of these studies I also acknowledge the generosity of the research funds of Hatfield Polytechnic.

The first Harris study involved a questionnaire survey of a systematic sample of the adult population and a study of pupils in primary and secondary schools. The secondary study included interviews with all the island's pupils in the top three secondary years at schools both on and off the island, following a 'verbal-guise test', described below. At the primary level, the percentage speaking Gaelic as their first language had decreased from 94% in 1957/58 to 67% in 1972/73, and it was clear that acquisition of English as a second language amongst the Gaelic-speakers was occurring readily before they started school. In terms of parental occupation and, the transmission of Gaelic to children, the most significant split occurred between the Skilled Manual and higher prestige groups on the one hand, and the Agricultural and other Manual groups on the other hand which maintained the higher levels of incidence of Gaelic.

Amongst the secondary-aged children, the verbal-guise test involved comparable speech samples in local colloquial Harris Gaelic, formal 'BBC' Gaelic, local Scottish English, and Received Pronunciation Standard English. The results were quite startling, with warm and supportive identifications being made with the Harris Gaelic speaker, and to some extent the others, except that very few respondents perceived the RP Standard English speaker in terms of generosity, kindness, likeability or honesty. This speaker was the one most respondents perceived as important, the best educated but he ranked only third in terms of cleverness. He was regarded as the least easy to understand, and by a very great margin the least desirable as a speech-model. The results of this verbal-guise test indicate the warmth with which local children regard the local community and its speech-ways, and the antipathy with which they have towards the language of social dominance – and by extension the structures which underlie it.

These reactions were generally shared by the non-Gaelic speaking children. At that time secondary schools were not attempting to make their non-Gaelic-speaking pupils effectively bilingual (although there were some successes in the primary schools), but nevertheless the non-Gaelic-speakers desired access to the local language and its associations. The school could be seen as neutral in this respect, although clearly it continued the Gaelic language-development for native speakers. In directing the brighter, abler pupils towards academic streaming and further education, essentially involving a move away from Harris, the education system could be seen as having a tacit function in shaping the size, internal structure and character of local society.

Amongst the adult population of Harris, this study examined the extent to which people used Gaelic and English for a substantial number of everyday speech situations. Gaelic was used very predominantly for such activities as speaking with family and relations, croft work, township meetings, personal prayer and conversations with church elders and missionaries. English very greatly perdominated in counting, dealings with doctors, travelling salesmen, bank staff, police, telephone operators and crofting assessors, and at public entertainments.

The study also asked a number of questions focusing on 'language-loyalty': the extent to which people feel a sense of affection for or commitment to their language. The results in terms of social identities were quite interesting. In occupational terms the agricultural group – the 'crofting core' of the community was substantially the most loyal towards Gaelic, with loyalty diminishing somewhat amongst the unemployed, 'housewife-only' and manual categories on the one hand and also amongst public servants and professional categories on the other. Least loyal towards Gaelic were the technical and commercial respondents. In terms of age older people were more language-loyal than younger, expectedly enough, and there were no significant differences between the sexes overall. However, in terms of age and sex taken school, with church ranking third (especially amongst older respondents). Radio and television were ranked next (especially amongst younger) followed by work, offical bodies and public entertainments. Younger respondents gave some importance to crofting, and least generally rated was shopping.

The Harris study was intended as sampling a 'typical' Gaelic community – but of course communities differ in their way-of-life in all sorts of ways. A few years later I was able to undertake a study which contrasted Protestant Harris with Catholic Barra, in comparison with migrant Gaelic communities in Cape Breton Island, Nova Scotia whose culture and religion still reflected the Hebridean communities which they had left five or six generations earlier. These areas were Catholic Broad Cove and Inverness, and Protestant Lake Ainslie, St. Ann's and the North Shore.

Although in these areas Gaelic was by the late '70s very much restricted to the older generation, the traditional culture was still very active, and the study also explored the extent to which its skills were still practised. Some aspects of the traditional culture were very much more alive than in Scotland, such as step-dancing and fiddle music. As in Scotland, the traditional cultural skills were very much kin-related together the younger women of child-rearing age were the least loyal towards Gaelic on these questions of all the age and gender-groups. This result if at all general throughout Gaelic communities has the most profound importance for the future of the language.

Respondents were also asked within which three everyday situations they would most wish Gaelic to be maintained. Most respondents cited home and

and almost entirely communicated within the family. The study asked a number of questions concerning 'cultural loyalty' as an extension of the 'language-loyalty' explored by the earlier study, and also sought details of ability to speak, read and write Gaelic, and the extent it was spoken in present-day and original family life.

In these communities, Gaelic was still strong amongst the elderly: 75% of over 65's claimed to be mother-tongue speakers. This generation had acquired their Gaelic in a still predominantly Gaelic rural community. Economic depression (*a' bhochd-ainn*) drove many out, as did the war, but rising prosperity helped some at least to stay. Although the ability to speak Gaelic was strongly age-related in Cape Breton, there were no differences between the sexes overall, except that in each sample on any definition of Gaelic-speaking ability the young women under 45 were significantly the least able of any age- and gender-group.

As in the earlier Harris study, the ability to speak Gaelic and attitudes towards the language and its culture were analysed in terms of social identities. In terms of occupation, Gaelic was strongest in the semi-skilled category which comprised the community core whose traditional way-of-life very much resembled crofting, combining small-scale agriculture with part-time jobs like logging and fishing, and semi-skilled work in construction and transport. As in the Western Isles, Gaelic was very much weaker amongst both the unskilled manual groups on the one hand and the more highly-skilled, managerial and professional groups on the other. These groups in both countries were more marginal to the strongly-

Gaelic crofter/small farmer community core of semi-
skilled occupations. By educational level, those fin-
ishing at grade school (Cape Breton) and elementary
school (Western Isles) were the most strongly Gaelic –
a clear age-related factor. The least strongly Gaelic
were those who had proceeded to technical and vocational education.

The Catholic communities and the Catholics in the
Protestant areas were the most retentive of their
Gaelic language and culture, closely followed by the
Presbyterians, which parallelled the situation in Barra
and Harris between Catholics and Free Presbyterians.
Traditional Gaelic literacy is very much influenced by
religious culture. In the Cape Breton samples only
four respondents claimed to have been taught Gaelic
at school, so any Gaelic literacy was either associated
with traditional religious practice, or the result of self-
education.

The Presbyterians were the most literate, as in the
Western Isles. Higher education – but not technical
or vocational education – seemed to have improved
Gaelic literacy as a by-product, and this was reflected
amongst occupational groups, as Gaelic literacy was
highest amongst the the semi-skilled 'core' compared
with the unskilled manual and more highly skilled
categories. None of the younger women was able to
read Gaelic.

In the Western Isles, Gaelic literacy was much
higher than in Cape Breton, and since Gaelic has
been taught in school over a much longer period,
ability to read and write Gaelic was much higher
amongst younger respondents. In terms of religious
culture, Gaelic reading ability was highest amongst
the Free Presbyterians, next highest amongst Free

Churchers, lower amongst Roman Catholics – and least amongst Church of Scotland attenders. Formal education, as in Cape Breton, also seems to have improved Gaelic literacy – as a by-product in most cases. Amongst occupational categories the highest levels were amongst the skilled non-manual and professional/managerial groups. The lower Gaelic literacy of the more 'marginal' skilled manual and unskilled categories follows the pattern in contrast with the higher Gaelic reading and writing abilities of the semi-skilled 'crofting core'.

Respondents were asked about the extent to which they used Gaelic and English in eleven everyday speech situations in their original and present families. In Cape Breton there had obviously been a greater language-shift in favour of English, but in both countries a similar pattern was apparent. Gaelic was better maintained in conversations with older people, and outside the home in the community. Gaelic was weakening in people's 'inner speech', and in worship, and in the Western Isles at public entertainments. Weakest of all were situations involving children.

These patterns of Gaelic speaking and reading abilities amongst age, sex groups and occupational and educational levels were very similar to the patterns of actual use of Gaelic in family life. In each of the four community samples, the extent to which Gaelic was actually used in both original and present families was very much age-related, as would be expected, but again in each case the younger women reported the lowest actual usage of Gaelic of all the age- and gender-groups. In the Western Isles the younger women also reported the greatest decline in using Gaelic between their original and present families. In Cape Breton this had occurred much earlier, and showed up amongst the middle-aged women instead.

It also signified the greatest extent of inter-generational decline in Gaelic usage. In both Cape Breton samples the younger women were the weakest in Gaelic usage of all the age and gender-groups. But this group did not show up as the greatest in terms of intergenerational decline, as for them this process had occurred much earlier, and decline in Gaelic usage was now proceding more rapidly amongst the middle-aged.

Nevertheless, the lesser inclination of the younger women actually to use their Gaelic, taken together with their reported lower Gaelic ability-levels, reinforces the concern for the future of the language as a mother-tongue.

In family and community life, Catholics and Presbyterians in both countries reported higher levels of actual use of their Gaelic than other religious groups. In Cape Breton the semi-skilled and skilled manual groups reported the highest levels of actual use of Gaelic of all the occupational categories, and in the Western Isles the semi-skilled and unskilled groups used their Gaelic most. Similarly by educational level, Gaelic was most in use amongst respondents educated only up to grade school (Cape Breton) and elementary levels (Western Isles), although this was chiefly an age and opportunity related factor. Younger respondents who had attended only to high school/junior secondary level were however very closely similar. The least inclined actually to use their Gaelic in family and community life were the technically and vocationally educated.

'Language-loyalty' towards Gaelic was generally much stronger amongst older respondents, but again there were no overall differences between the sexes, except that the younger women under 45 were significantly the least 'loyal' towards Gaelic of all the age and gender-groups. Taken together with how they rated their use of and ability to speak Gaelic, their less-supportive attitudes towards the language must further weaken its maintenance in the upbringing of children.

The older respondents who did not get a secondary education were the most loyal to Gaelic in each of the four communities studied, but in more strictly educational terms, educational levels leading to technical and vocational careers were associated with the lower levels of Gaelic 'language-loyalty'.

The survey also studied the possession of of traditional Gaelic entertainment skills (such as instrumental music, singing, dancing and storytelling). Their patterning in terms of people's social identity, was very similar to people's language abilities and attitudes described above, except that these cultural skills were best represented amongst Catholics, and least amongst Presbyterians.

Like the language factors the possession of cultural skills increased with age. There were no differences between the sexes as such, except that again taking age and gender together the younger women under fourty-five were the least skilled in the traditional entertainment culture. This was true both in Cape Breton and in the less traditionally entertainment-skilled case of Harris. In Barra these skills were better distributed across age-groups, suggesting that Gaelic culture is more lively there. The transmission of the traditional culture seemed to be very much a family affair. Everyone reporting such skills, reported them also in their families, and the most versatile came from the most versatile families. Once again, the technical, vocational and higher education groups were the weakest in the possession of these cultural skills.

As might be expected, people's loyalty to Gaelic culture closely resembled the patterning of language-loyalty. Loyalty to the traditional Gaelic entertainment culture was highest amongst Catholics and lowest amongst Presbyterians in both countries. Cultural loyalty increased with age but did not did not differ greatly between the sexes, although taking both factors together, the younger women under forty-five again proved the least supportive of Gaelic culture. Loyalty towards Gaelic culture was however very strong amongst the more highly educated Gaelic-speakers in both Cape Breton and the Western Isles surveys, and closely matched the high levels of cultural loyalty amongst the older respondents who did not get a secondary education. In occupational terms cultural loyalty was highest within the 'crofting core' of the community and local professional groups, and lowest amongst technical, vocational and skilled manual groups.

The social identities within the *Gàidhealtachd* which have proved to be the most supportive of the language and its culture have been the traditional crofter category with whom have been associated semi-skilled manual trades. But the more highly educated group of professionally-educated Gaelic-speaking ministers, teachers and nurses can be a strength in the community also – despite their relatively small numbers –

since they carry social prestige. The occupational group which has seemed to be the least supportive has been the 'notorious social class three' (skilled manual and non-manual occupations), which has been described in a similar study in Wales (Harrison, et al., 1981) as the class 'most on the make' and most instrumental in its attitudes.

Until recently Gaelic has not featured greatly in Scottish further education (in business colleges, technical and vocational institutions) as it has for many years in colleges of education and the universities. Economic and cultural factors have thus combined to depress support for the language. Such attitudes have disparaged the language for its supposed lack of economic value. But such attitudes now have to face growing demand and job opportunities for Gaelic – and since 1983 it has been possible to get a business education through Gaelic.

Migration, particularly of younger women, is particularly high in Gaelic communities. The young men are enabled to inherit the croft or a share in a boat or a small business, thereby securing an economic basis for the future family. The more able young women have to seek their prospects elsewhere, depressing the local balance of the sexes amongst young adults. The media dubbed these cases 'islands of bachelors', in the wake of studies which had drawn attention to this problem.

Young Gaelic-speaking men often have to seek elsewhere for a wife, who will very typically not be Gaelic-speaking. Family and community life then turns over from Gaelic to English – a situation which is now commonly being observed particularly in some smaller Hebridean communities and islands.

If these surveys were at all representative of the
Gaelic community as a whole, it is clear that the shift
away from Gaelic towards English is very strongly
linked with specific social identities and economic
processes, as had been seen in the Harris study some
years earlier, and has been borne out in more recent
studies of Skye and the Western Isles as a whole. The
younger women who remain in these communities
have shown up as a very crucial group for the future
of Gaelic, since amongst them are the mothers of the
next generation of Gaelic speakers.

Other studies of language in the British Isles have
shown similar tendencies of younger women in working-class communities to model themselves upon the
speakers of middle-class accents and standard English. The young women who go in for careers based
on higher and further education which take them
away from the Gaelic communities may perhaps not
share the same attitudes – although they will have
very largely to live their lives through the medium of
English. It is the young women who remain behind in
their home communities who seem to have the less-
supportive attitudes to their mother-tongue and culture. Perhaps they hope to rise socially and marry
'upwards'. If they do not, and marry locally their less-
supportive attitudes towards Gaelic may then be reflected in their family life.

Young women who have moved away from the
Gàidhealtachd for education or employment are often
amongst the most supportive of their Gaelic mother-
tongue and native culture. The young mothers
amongst them, who have made their careers and
families away from the *Gàidhealtachd*, have organised
playgroups and have demanded Gaelic-medium edu-

cation for their children. This has produced, in the '80's the most encouraging prospects for the future of Gaelic – starting from bases such as Glasgow and Inverness. Gaelic playgroups and Gaelic-medium schooling are now vigorously spreading back into the Gaelic areas – and are even getting over into Cape Breton.

A study of this development was undertaken by Anne Lorne Gillies, then Education Officer of *CnaG*, and for some years a very active patron of the CNSA, the Gaelic Playgroups Association, as her doctoral study at Glasgow University, reporting in 1989. In outlining her study she says, 'Recent developments are fully described, with family case-studies, classroom observations, a detailed survey of popular attitudes towards Gaelic education, and a survey and statistical analysis of the extra-mural Gaelic exposure of all children attending Gaelic-medium Primary Units throughout Scotland in 1989.'

Of her principal findings amongst a survey of Gaelic-speakers throughout Scotland, Dr. Gillies says that, 'Popular attitudes proved extremely positive, with large majorities of the sample in full support of Gaelic- medium teaching at pre-school, primary and secondary levels, and acknowledging the vital importance of the mainstream education system in language maintenance among today's young people. This opinion gains credence from research results which show an alarming lack of exposure to Gaelic in the community and, in many cases, the home – even in the linguistic heartland. Official endorsement of Gaelic teaching, it seems, is not merely symbolically important: it may be the only way for the language to survive.'

Amongst her principal conclusions, Dr Gillies says that, 'The recent establishment of Gaelic-medium education programmes in urban centres such as Inverness, Glasgow and Edinburgh – and very positive popular response to these measures – implies that (a) Gaelic is of interest and relevance to the whole of Scotland, including its centres of industry and commerce, not merely to a hitherto retreating rural heartland and (b) that Gaelic/English bilingualism has potential as an additive and stable phenomenon, as opposed to being replacive and transitional. The research uncovered a strong sense among non-Gaelic speaking parents, even those with no discernible or recent Gaelic-speaking ancestry, of historical dislocation from a vital part of their cultural heritage.

The education system is commonly seen as the principal culprit in this, and is looked to to redress the balance. Correspondingly, the production of a new generation of urban second-language Gaelic-speaking children, of non-Highland parentage, requires us to redefine the 'Gaelic community' within Scotland and identify appropriate measures to service the phenomenon and maintain its momentum... Thus the development of Gaelic-medium education in response to parental demand outwith the residual heartland may be seen as offering a means of expression to a hitherto unfocused sense of Scottish ethnicity.'

Of the reasons for past efforts at language revival foundering, Dr Gillies cites, '...the tendency for campaigns to be generated from outwith, and with little attempt to involve or inform, the grassroots Gaelic community; their failure to address underly-

ing social and economic problems within that community; the respectable caution of their terms of
reference...the   argument...that   teaching   Gaelic
speakers through the medium of their native language is, if nothing else, the most effective route to the
introduction of English. Thus the underlying assumption appears to be that education is, ultimately,
designed to fit the people for migration, as the only
real solution to the socio-economic problems of the
Highlands... Arguably the events of the last decade or
so (the creation of the Western Isles Islands Council,
its Gaelic bilingual policy, the establishment of *Comhairle nan Sgoiltean Araich* – the Gaelic Play-group
Association – and *Comunn na Gàidhlig*, and the growth
of parental demand for mainstream Gaelic-medium
education) have been more significant in terms of
language regeneration than those of the century pre-
ceding them.

These events have been typified by grassroots
involvement... are apolitical, parent-generated, and
based to a large extent on the pragmatic premise:
'why should children be monolingual when they obviously are capable of being bilingual?''

The national public opinion survey on attitudes towards Gaelic language policies undertaken in 1981
was the first of its kind ever undertaken – and there
has only been one other case of public opinion questions on Gaelic being reported in the press since. The
1981 survey was carried out on much the same lines
as surveys on political and general issues reported in
the press, but special attention was given to Gaelic
areas such as the Western Isles, Skye and the mainland Highlands. The survey asked about the extent of

support for various policies concerning Gaelic in the media, education and public life. As expected, support was strongest in the Western Isles, decreasing in Skye and the mainland Highlands, and least in the Lowlands. Although support amongst Gaelic speakers was strong, the most supportive group of all were Gaelic learners, and even those with only a smattering of the language and those with Gaelic-speaking relatives registered much higher levels of support than the remainder.

In the Lowland area support for Gaelic policies increased with age, with no overall difference between the sexes. However in the more strongly Gaelic areas of the Western Isles the younger women significantly registered the lowest levels of support amongst age and gender-groups, in line with previous studies. In the more strongly Gaelic areas, support for Gaelic policies was strongest amongst the semi and unskilled manual categories and weakest amongst the professional and managerial categories. In the Lowlands this pattern was reversed. Voting intentions were also very clearly associated with extent of support for Gaelic policies. In every area the highest support came from Nationalist voters – even in Skye where the typical voter had been Liberal, and the Western Isles where there was a higher proportion of Gaelic speakers amongst Labour voters. Conservative voters were everywhere the least supportive, (except in the Western Isles where the least supportive were minor party supporters, 'don't knows' and non-voters.) Overall, as in the Lowland sample, political support for Gaelic policies fell on a continuum from most to least supportive from S.N.P., minor parties, Alliance parties, Labour, no clear voting intention, to Conservative.

The survey asked sixteen questions on attitudes towards Gaelic or opinions on Gaelic language policies. On the whole the results seemed to indicate no great opposition or enmity towards Gaelic, as has often been supposed, but rather on some questions a degree of unawareness or even indifference. There were generally moderate levels of support for most of the issues nationally, but the results for the question on Gaelic in schools was the most encouraging, as was that relating to programmes for Gaelic learners on radio and television. Interestingly, the highest agreement response of all was on ever having seen or heard a Gaelic programme (– and indeed during the '70s Gaelic music programmes had been attracting audiences of between 500,000 – 800,000). Most of the questions produced majorities in favour of Gaelic policies in conventional opinion poll terms, i.e. eliminating 'don't knows'.

In some cases there was quite a difference between these percentages and the percentages of the whole sample agreeing with the statement, where it would seem that the issue was being raised for the first time within the Lowland context. The results are of some interest as a record of public opinion on Gaelic issues at the time, and as they have some implications for Gaelic policy-making they are summarised in the Appendix.

The results of the survey undertaken throughout the main Gaelic-speaking areas of Skye and the Western Isles between 1985-88 have not yet been fully published. As already indicated they do bear out, with larger samples and across a wider area, the main conclusions of the earlier surveys in Barra and

Harris. The study also undertook a detailed analysis of census returns for Gaelic. These showed up a number of important features. Some results of the improvement in provision of Gaelic in primary education were quite apparent.

Wherever Gaelic had featured in any way in primary education, a census increase of Gaelic speakers had occurred amongst school-aged children and young people. This upturn was also apparent from 1971, ten years before a similar upturn had been visible for Welsh for which there had been a considerable amount of educational development.

The increase of Gaelic-speakers in Highland Perthshire, where the language was moribund, can be related specifically to the areas in which these schemes operated, and to the age-groups which were involved. The national increase in numbers and proportions of Gaelic speakers in these age-groups can also be shown specifically to relate to those areas in which primary Gaelic teaching schemes operated. Conversely, those areas without such schemes clearly show the decline of the language in keeping with long-term trends.

In interpreting these results, it must be remembered that the population census is essentially a self-report exercise, and in the case of children what we have are their parents' beliefs regarding their linguistic ability. In many areas where the language is weak, parents may be regarding fairly modest levels of Gaelic ability as qualifying for census entry. The census does not require any assessment of level of language abilties. At the most cautious level however, the results can indicate a measure of parental goodwill for Gaelic, and an endorsement of the provision of Gaelic in their children's schools.

The increase in Gaelic primary teaching schemes during the '60s and '70s can thus show results. The increases of Gaelic speakers in these age-groups were in any case not only greater than overall change in numbers, but moreover related only to those areas where Gaelic was taught. Elsewhere, the numbers of Gaelic-speaking young people declined both relatively and absolutely.

The position of Gaelic in recent decades has thus not been entirely a case of irreversible decline. The numbers and proportions of Gaelic speakers had declined at every census and virtually in every area from 1891 to 1961. But between 1961-71, the overall number and proportion increased nationally for the first time, although this effect was in fact produced in the Lowland – or 'non-Gaelic-speaking' area. Between 1971-81, although numbers and proportions declined nationally to around the 1961 level, for the first time ever there were numerical and proportional increases in Gaelic speakers in the main Gaelic- speaking areas of the Western Isles and parts of Skye. Similar increases also occurred in Ross & Cromarty, the Moray Firth area, Highland Perthshire and suburban areas around Glasgow. In the more strongly Gaelic- speaking areas the age-groups producing this increase were the young adults and schoolchildren.

Oil-related developments were attracting workers to the Moray Firth area, but also to the areas around Kishorn in Wester Ross and Arnish in Lewis, where rig-fabrication yards had been established. A study of this last case (Prattis, 1980) found that it had the effect of attracting Gaelic-speaking workers back to

Lewis, and strengthening Gaelic in the work situation and community life. The 1981 Census indicated numerical and proportional increases in Gaelic speakers in Lewis amongst young adults and children. The Kishorn fabrication yard closed in 1988, and Arnish in 1989, and with them any spin-off which they may have had for the local economy and prospects for Gaelic regeneration.

At the 1981 Census, the Gaelic population had on the whole been an ageing sector of the population – but the increase in Gaelic speaking abilities amongst older children and young adults had produced a 'bulge' in the population profile. This was a feature only of the most strongly Gaelic-speaking areas, and particularly those areas with primary Gaelic teaching schemes. The population profile of Gaelic speakers in the Lowland area remained greatly attenuated in the age-ranges of childhood and youth.

It remains to be seen whether the gains for Gaelic related to oil-developments will persist in the 1991 census, and whether the developments in Gaelic-medium education will become apparent.

At the 1981 census there were areas within Skye and the Western Isles in which the proportion of young people (aged 5-24) speaking Gaelic matched or exceeded the proportion in the older age-ranges. These areas could be said to show some viability in their maintenance of the language. They comprised nine of the fifty enumeration districts in Skye, chiefly in its extremities; and thirty of the 140 enumeration districts of the Western Isles, chiefly in western Lewis, southern Harris, Uist and Barra. Using as an alternative measure of viability the proportion of the local Gaelic-speaking population aged under twenty-five, and thus the potential parents of the next generation, there were five enumeration districts in Skye and forty-one in the Western Isles where this age-group was over 30% of all Gaelic speakers. Amongst these were areas close to such anglicising centres as Broadford, Stornoway and the military installations in Benbecula and South Uist.

Thus in 1981 there were still local neighbourhoods throughout Skye and the Western Isles which were maintaining Gaelic and reproducing themselves as viable Gaelic speech-communities even on the very strictest of criteria. Moreover, this had occurred without the level of official protection and subsidisation undertaken in the Irish Gaeltacht. The Gaelic communities have surprisingly maintained themselves into the late 20th Century despite the most formidable adversities. Those in earlier history were considered in Part I. The modern history of Gaelic society since the Clearances and the establishment of the crofting community, has included two world wars, a profound intervening depression, and a subsequent history of both neglect and exploitation with little regard for community and ecological values. Sporadic development has occurred, and economic collapse has followed. The oil boom came – and suddenly went – with fish-farming perhaps to follow. Development agencies, it is fair to say, have tried to take advantage of these trends and mitigate their after-effects. They have even begun to find a place for Gaelic amongst them.

Details on age and sex of Gaelic speakers first became available with the 1921 census results, and show most dramatically the literal 'bite' which war had taken out of the younger men of the Gaelic com-

munity compared with the rest of the population. In
Lewis this was followed by heavy emigration to Canada. The second world war did not bear so heavily
upon the Gaelic population as cannon-fodder, but
attrition of the population continued. Migration of
young people from the Gaelic areas remained high –
and analysis reveals this to be higher amongst young
women than young men. On the other hand, analysis
of the data for qualifications and employment by age
and sex in the Gaelic island areas indicates that there
is a greater 'reverse-flow' of the more highly- quali-
fied women than men back into these areas – often
without the prospect of employment.

Research can thus demonstrate some viability for
the Gaelic community, and show how the language
has been maintained amongst its speakers. It has also
shown what effects social and economic processes
have had upon the speech-community and its ability
to transmit its language and culture to the younger
generation. Can these findings be effectively applied
in enabling the Gaelic community to make it into the
21st Century?

STRATEGIES FOR SURVIVAL

The increase in Gaelic speakers amongst young people noted in the last two censuses related to about half of the school catchment areas in the Highlands and Hebrides, where there were schemes for teaching Gaelic as a second language, or bilingually as a teaching medium together with English. Until 1985 there were no primary Gaelic teaching schemes outwith the Highlands and Islands, and neither were there any Gaelic-medium units – teaching the whole curriculum throughout the primary stage through the medium of Gaelic – anywhere. It might be wondered what the effects might have been in the 1981 census results had there been a more widespread availablilty of Gaelic in primary education.

The presence and status of Gaelic in the local educational system undoubtedly assists its stabilisation in the community, and the development of effective

Gaelic-speaking ability through playgroups and Gaelic-medium units must assist language-maintenance and regeneration. Even the development of literacy itself may assist in this process. Colin Baker's study 'Aspects of Bilingualism in Wales' (1984) presents census analysis supporting this for Welsh. Detailed analysis of the 1981 Census small area statistics in Scotland indicates a similar correlation between high levels of Gaelic literacy and local community language-maintenance.

Also in Wales, Geraint Williams of University College Aberystwyth Department of Geography has estimated that where the incidence of Welsh falls below 70%, local communities tend to switch to English in everyday life. Unless the advances for Gaelic in education are matched by opportunities to use the language in everyday life, including the communications media, the future is not secured. It is doubtful whether the language could be effectively maintained solely by a network of isolated families and individuals without actual communities using it as the chief means of communication in everyday life.

Another factor crucially affects the provision of Gaelic in the schools. Demand is high – perhaps surprisingly so. Supply of registered teachers is limited. Despite government promises to respond to the wishes of parents and to the articulated wishes of the Gaelic community as a whole, the progress of Gaelic in the education system is being held back by the lack of suitably trained and available registered teachers. In 1988 there was a threat to reorganise Celtic Studies within the university system, and to run the Gaelic/bilingual teaching method course in Bachelor of Education and Postgraduate Certificate courses between

Jordanhill at Glasgow and Northern College at Aberdeen in alternate years.

These changes could have cut down the supply of Gaelic teachers at source. Fortunately, the Universities Funding Council was persuaded to retain Celtic Studies at Aberdeen, Edinburgh and Glasgow, and the Scottish Education Department to enable both Northern College, and Jordanhill to continue to offer Gaelic. It is also offered at St Andrew's College, Bearsden.

Education authorities have often tended to feel that students from 'their' own home areas proceeding to teacher training and returning as 'home region students' should properly be committed to pursuing their career for the authority which has exclusively 'invested' in them. Trained teachers going elsewhere in the system for career purposes are thus seen as 'loss'. The concept of a national Gaelic education service has not always been the most salient image in the vision of directors and conveners of education. Schools' career advice has not always encouraged pupils to make a career in Gaelic education – and to be fair, the uncertainties in this field have made it prudent for a teacher to qualify for another specialism in addition to Gaelic.

The developing links between education authorities leading to the recent establishment of the Inter-Authority Standing Group on Gaelic Education may be seen as the first step towards a co- ordinated Gaelic education service in which there will be some forward planning of personnel and resource requirements, and effective liaison with teacher education and accreditation. There are also the Inter-Authority Primary and Secondary Review Groups, advisers who meet to co-ordinate various projects and matters of common concern. Effective recruitment to a Gaelic education service can only occur if a careers' structure is created and can be perceived by and recommended to intending teachers in school and higher education.

There is an urgent role for the General Teaching Council in reviewing what is required for the registration of teachers not only of Gaelic as a subject, but of teachers using Gaelic as a teaching medium – at all stages and for all aspects of the curriculum. The rapid pace of developments in Gaelic education has begun to overtake the structures and concepts based on previous practice.

Educational policies on languages in Scottish schools were discussed in Chapter 10. The place of Gaelic in the school curriculum has improved, but its status is still far from satisfactory in official pronouncements. The 'National Curriculum' developed under the 1988 Educational Reform Act does not apply to Scotland, and it is often asserted – sometimes officially – that Scotland has no national curriculum. The facts are that Scotland is rapidly and tacitly acquiring one, often 'by the back door' and all too often as a copy of England's. This of course inevitably takes Scottish practice further away from the rest of Europe, and further isolates our educational institutions. In May 1989 Kenneth Baker, the English Secretary of State for Education, at Brussels took Scotland as well as England out of the E.C. LINGUA programme which would have greatly assisted languages teaching and overseas exchanges in primary and secondary schools.

Baker's pretext in refusing to adopt a curriculum policy of two 'other languages' was that so many chil-

dren in Britain's schools needed to learn an ethnic
minority language. Only in Wales is a language other
than English placed within the 'core curriculum' –
and in England any parallels between the place of
Welsh and ethnic minority languages was expressly
repudiated. It would be good to see Scottish education taking the initiative to create a policy for language as such within the curriculum, in place of
piecemeal policies for English, 'modern foreign languages', and 'Gaelic, Asian and Classical languages'.
The experience of Gaelic-medium and bilingual education has been similar to that of Welsh: effective
acquistion of a second language must start in the
primary school.

Bilingual education with a free choice between
Gaelic, 'modern foreign languages' and ethnic minority languages should be available to all, with opportunity for a second 'other language' at the secondary
stage. The successes of Gaelic education would thus
have a wider application, minority languages would
gain real justice instead of being used as a pretext,
and our language policies would be an advance upon
LINGUA.

Analysis of census results and the findings of evaluative studies indicate that investment in Gaelic education is effective. Education is a key field for language-
regeneration, and has a stabilising and strengthening
effect in community life. However, the broadening-
out of the population structures of Gaelic speakers as
Gaelic is effectively acquired by school pupils is
unfortunately counteracted by the contraction of the
Gaelic-speaking population amongst young to
middle-aged adults. The regenerative effect of education becomes dispersed as young people migrate. A

number of strategies could be envisaged in overcoming these effects.

An immediate objective might be the creation of a Gaelic women's organisation. In Wales a successful Welsh-language women's organisation, *Merched y Wawr* (Daughters of 'The Dawn' – named from a popular Welsh women's magazine) was founded in 1967 following the refusal of the Women's Institute in Wales to permit the use of Welsh in its meetings and their business. In the Scottish *Gàidhealtachd*, the Women's Rural Institute is, like other national voluntary organisations, a strongly anglicising organisation. The Scout and Guide Movement, the Boys' and Girls' Brigades, and youth clubs generally have had a strongly anglicising presence. The recent creation of '*sradagan*' – youth clubs for both the primary and teens age-ranges – has been a countervailing strategy promoted by *CnaG* since 1987.

Whether national voluntary organisations, which are generally directed from London – or at least from Lowland Scotland – could ever be pursuaded to engage in a more Gaelic profile is highly questionable. They have always been run through English, and might complain that a Gaelic or even a bilingual profile was 'linguistically divisive'. A Gaelic women's organisation linked to a Gaelic women's journal could, as in Wales, probably do a great deal more effectively to utilise the commitment and enthusiasm for the language which is evident amongst many women and overcome inimical attitudes towards the language amongst others. CNSA has effectively promoted parent groups, which have formed a co-ordinated linkage as 'Pàrantan airson Foghlaim Gàidhlig' (Parents for Gaelic Education).

The dispersal of the Gaelic-speaking population at the 1981 Census can be gauged by the proportion of Gaelic speakers living in neighbourhoods (census enumeration districts) where Gaelic was spoken by the majority (50% or more) of the local population, and in those where the language was spoken by 75% or more (– the level at which the language can be truly said to function as community speech).

Analysis of census small area statistics indicated that only 27,813 of Scotland's 79,307 Gaelic speakers lived in neighbourhoods in which Gaelic was spoken by a majority of the population: just over one in three or 34.9% of the total. Truly Gaelic neighbourhoods, where 75% or more spoke the language, were home to 20,345 – just over one in four or 25.7% of all Gaelic speakers. The language can only thus potentially re-produce itself from these areas, and they are home only to between one-third and one-quarter of the total speech-community. Any effective strategy for survival must take account of this pattern of dispersal. It is also quite naive to regard any increase of Gaelic speakers amongst young people as in itself automati-cally ensuring the future.

In strengthening the economic base of local com-munities, the danger for the prospects of Gaelic being maintained as community speech lies in economic opportunity pulling in substantial numbers of non-Gaelic-speakers who will decisively change the speechways of the locality. In southern Skye local post-offices and shops have been bought by incomers from the south – and almost at a stroke Gaelic has ceased to be the language of shopping. In Glendale in northern Skye, where crofters had been able to pur-chase their crofts by annuity and had thus since 1955 acquired the right to sell their freeholds, the turnover of local population has fundamentally changed the local culture of one of the redoubts of the crofting system. The Western Isles are still largely insulated from these changes by their remoteness, and the crofting system has been an important factor in maintaining community life and acting as a 'gatekeeper' against intrusive outsider settlement.

Census analysis can also demonstrate the strength of the correlation between community involvement in crofting and the maintenance of Gaelic. The crofting system, a low level of local economic development, and a high level of migration have meant that in successive generations those who have stayed have just about been able to secure a local home. In areas such as North Wales and the English Lake District the local housing market has rocketed out of the reach of ordinary local young people.

Since the Crofting Reform (Scotland) Act of 1976 all crofters have had the right to buy their crofts and to sell them on the open market. It is remarkable how comparatively few crofters have taken advantage of this, but if crofting areas become subject to pressure of incomer demand as in Wales and the Lake District, the crofting system could probably not for very long withstand it.

After the First World War, returning soldiers who had fought with the promises of 'homes fit for heroes' and 'two acres and a cow', found the promises hollow. Little had happened except a relaxation of building regulations to make self-building a little easier. So in the Gàidhealtachd self-build they did. Farms and estates of absentee landlords were raided and crofting settlements established. In Harris the last of these

settlements was Seilebost, established in the early '30s
by Bays families from the infertile east coast. After
the Second World War, similar homesteading occurred in 1948 – this time from the cities – in Knoydart
and Wester Ross. It was on a smaller scale, local
people were not involved, and the impetus quickly
petered out.

A similar strategy for Highland or Gaelic regeneration which has been floated recently has been the
acquisition of Highland estates by the HIDB. Strath,
North Harris and Knoydart, which were for sale in
recent years, would have been ideal. Their development for Gaelic homesteading could have been constituted as *'co-chomainn'*, with HIDB assistance, and
their position further secured by Crofters' Commission powers. Instead, such estates are bartered on an
international market and all too typically come to be
run merely for sporting interests or asset-stripping by
outsiders or foreign syndicates. There have however
been instances of benevolent landlordism. For
example, *Fearann Eilean Iarmain*, the former Macdonald Estate in Skye, was acquired by Iain Noble
around 1971 and has been run with some consideration for the local community and culture, using Gaelic
as the language of business management and economic development. Nearby, Strath – the former
MacKinnon Estate – was acquired by Ian Anderson
(of the Jethro Tull rock group) and has been run
more for food and its folk than for the gun. There is
also the example of Scoraig. A deserted township on
Little Loch Broom in Wester Ross, approachable only
by boat or over rough moorland, was settled by
incomers attempting self-sufficiency and a generally
Green philosophy. The skills and educational experi-

ence of the parents enabled them to establish their own school, and by 1989 they had secured an arrangement to run their own secondary school so their children did not have to board away at Ullapool.

So far nothing like this has been attempted in the spirit of Gaelic homesteading – but the west coast abounds in remote and deserted crofting townships. The potential is there. This is the succesful model of the Jewish Kibbutzim, which restored Hebrew as a vernacular, first in Europe in the late 19th Century through the leadership of Eliezer Ben-Yehuda – and then in the 20th century laid the foundation for David Ben-Gurion's vision of a Hebrew-speaking working-class in Israel. The tradition of homesteading, as well as the administrative structures and powers for such a policy in Scotland already exist. They have only partially been used. Crofting, co-chomainn and homesteading could be brought together into a '*Coimhearsnachd Ghàidhealach*' a 'Highland Community' – with a difference: its purpose would be to regenerate community values through the medium of the Gaelic language.

Such a 'neo-Gaeltacht' had been mooted in the Republic of Ireland in an urban context: *Buaic* was one such attempt – and *Na Teaghlachtai Gaelachai* was another, promoting a national network of Irish-speaking families. The successful implementation of this idea actually came about in Northern Ireland, in West Belfast. Gabrielle Maguire, who has researched language-revival in this community, observes: 'The history of the Irish language verifies the ... statement by Dorian, 'The home is the last bastion of a subordinate language in competition with a dominant language...' Founder members of the Shaw's Road

Community in Belfast decided to use the home as the first bastion of the Irish language, from where it would be propelled into other domains. They established a company which would negociate loans and secure a site. Members built their own homes. The first family took up residence in 1969.' They have now had for some years their own Irish-language primary school, drawing children in from beyond the community. Such developments in an urban or rural context would be quite feasible in Scotland: a Gaelic Shaw's Road or a Gaelic Scoraig.

The viability of existing Gaelic communities and the creation of new ones must be considered essential in any strategy to maintain the Gaelic language as community speech. Yet the geographical distribution of Gaelic speakers throughout Scotland is such that policies implemented only in the Gaelic areas would benefit only a minority of Gaelic speakers.

Gaelic is not merely a Scottish language, it is unique to Scotland, and as history shows us it was in fact the original language of the Scottish people. It has claims to be recognised at the level of a national institution. Provision for the cultural needs of its speakers should therefore exist at a national level.

In the broadcasting media, there are four terrestrial channels and thirteen satellite channels presently available, and there are plans for a fifth terrestrial channel. Current proposals to fund a Gaelic television service for a further 200 hours annually, in addition to the current total, around 100 hours, will produce a daily output of under 1 hour of Gaelic programming. When this is set against the total of a daily output of around 250 hours of television from all current sources, under half a percent (0.4%) of all television

programming time in Scotland will be dedicated to
Gaelic. Its generosity is actually quite modest.

There are five BBC U.K. radio channels broadcasting in Scotland, plus Radio Scotland and its local 'opt-
outs', independent radio stations in the main centres
and the BBC World Service. As the government fran-
chises new 'community' radio stations, is it too much
to ask that one channel might be allocated for an all-
Gaelic service on the lines of Radio *Cymru* in Wales?
The BBC is prepared to devote one of its five
'national' channels almost exclusively to the musical
tastes of a tiny cultural and social elite. Radio Three
listening figures in Scotland are often much less than
those for the Gaelic services. If it is thought to be
inequitable to allocate a whole channel to only 80,000
Gaelic speakers, the U.K. Government nevertheless
funds a radio and television channel for a similar
number of English-speakers in Germany through the
British Forces Network. Their situation and their
distinctive cultural needs are very similar to those of
Gaelic speakers in Scotland.

Were the Gaelic populations of Lowland cities to be
regarded as 'islands' in their own right, they would
form a 'Gaelic Archipelago' as strongly Gaelic in
character as the Hebrides. Which they would be if
they were true communities. Socially they are in fact
composed of networks in which Gaelic speakers may
come together for specific purposes from time to
time, but in which Gaelic speakers are interacting for
the most part with others through the medium of
English.

Once there was a thriving 'Highland' culture in
places like Glasgow, with its season of Highland and
Gaelic functions run by 'territorial associations' cater-

ing for people from every area in the Highlands and
Islands. You could speak Gaelic any evening you
liked in the Highlanders' Institute. Unfortunately
that closed in 1979, and now if it's Gaelic 'crack' you
are after, you will need to seek out a pub like the Park
Bar or a Sunday service at St. Columba's. The Gaels
have moved out into the suburbs, and the territorial
associations have felt the pinch. What sort of institution could now take their place, and provide for the
cultural and entertainment needs for urban Gaels?

This deserves to be taken seriously as it affects
children and young people as well as adults. Since this
was first drafted, an appeal has gone out for just such
a cultural centre to be established in Glasgow.

Provision of cultural support in the 'Gaelic Archipelago' may be a lot easier for the Gaelic arts establishment to tackle than the task of providing for the
even more dispersed Gaelic speakers in the traditional *Gàidhealtachd* of the mainland Highlands. It is
probably still the case that every district – almost
every parish – within the 'Highland Line' still has
surviving native Gaelic speakers, even if of the oldest
generation. The last traditional Aberdeenshire Gaelic
speaker of Braemar – east of the Highland line – died
only a couple of years ago. The 'Gaelic Penumbra' of
the eastern and central Highlands is however streng-
thened by Gaelic speakers moving from further west.
In 1981 an area around Inverness similar in extent to
the Isle of Skye (northern Inverness District and
Easter Ross) contained more Gaelic speakers than the
Isle of Skye: 5040 as against 4303. Such local cluster-
ing makes provision for the Gaelic arts more economic. Some sort of Gaelic social or cultural centre
becomes a possibility too – a feasibility study for such

a centre in Inverness was undertaken by a *Sabhal Mór Ostaig* student in 1986, taking a Gaelic-orientated catering establishment in Crieff as a model.

The policies of *CnaG* consist of a multi-pronged strategy involving active lobbying and liaison with government departments and official bodies, the education system, and broadcasting authorities. It has mounted its own initiatives in youth work and the arts. In its review of its first five years' operation (Gaelic Progress Report 1982- 1988) *CnaG* has identified areas requiring critical attention. In Gaelic education these are the provision of resources including professional staff, and publicity drawing parents attention to new opportunities. In broadcasting the provision of adequate Gaelic services on radio and television still needs to be secured. In the commercial sphere – an area which has not yet been greatly involved in shouldering its reponsibilities towards the language – *CnaG* is hoping to appoint a development officer both to stimulate organisations to make more use of Gaelic, and to promote sales of Gaelic-related material.

There is no doubt that in *CnaG* the Gaelic cause has acquired an able and professional promotional body. In the first five years of its existence it has established a recognised profile for Gaelic in many quarters which count. It has established practical working groups which have utilised voluntary ability, and it has implemented its policies especially for the key sector of youth most effectively. Having proved itself, it deserves to be more adequately resourced in order to carry out its work on the scale necessary to provide the infrastructure without which Gaelic cannot hope to survive. There is still an unresolved 'grey area' in

the relationship between *CnaG* and *An Comunn Gàidhealach*, which could lead to dissipation of effort. Such
overlaps need to be resolved. The government would
wish to see the two bodies merged but there is probably a distinctive role for each still to play. *An Comunn*
has almost a century of experience as a voluntary
cultural organisation, and without it there would be
no *Mòd*. The *Cor na Gàidhlig* Report called for an
alternative and non-competitive Gaelic festival, but
the *Mòd* would still continue as a national institution
and would still need someone to run it. Although
CnaG is officially recognised and largely funded from
the public purse, it nevertheless has private members,
and as a limited company it has shareholders. It is
therefore not exactly a quango. If it were to develop
into something like the Welsh Language Board, there
would need to be a representative voluntary body to
keep it on its toes. Could *An Comunn* ever do that?
However, the reliance upon public funding may at
times have an inhibiting effect upon intervention in
public issues. The closure of small rural schools is
greatly inimical to the prospects for Gaelic in education and in the community. *CnaG* has been criticised
for not making its views more strongly known on the
matter..

On re-reading the final chapter of *The Lion's
Tongue*, which I wrote as a 'post-script' to the book in
1974, I asked a number of questions 'when?' The
answers came very swiftly over the few years which
followed. We have seen the first public demonstration, the first court case, the establishment of a youth
organisation, Gaelic on roadsigns, and improvements
in broadcasting. I thought we had 'only some five
years before the last Gaelic-speaking generation of

schoolchildren ceases to pass through our schools' in which to do something decisive in the educational sphere. And that the impending reform of local government presented unique opportunities. The early '70s seemed to me to be 'watershed years' for the language. And so they have proved to be!

The book therefore ended on an optimistic note: 'There is little time in which to act but the circumstances are not yet impossible for Gaelic, its speakers and its culture to be retained as a living whole. The dream of the return of the children of the Gael to repossess their own lands and their own cultural heritage may yet be capable of realisation.'

At the time I felt the optimism could be justified if the challenge were met – and in many ways over the past sixteen years the opportunities have been seized. There has even been a 'reverse-flow' of young Gaels coming back into the Gaelic areas for developing opportunities not only in the boom-and-bust oil-industries, but into better secured prospects in public administration, business management, education and the media. These young people are able, well-educated, and confident in their culture. Above all, they see some future for themselves and their families in their home areas. They are opinion-formers, decision-makers and community-leaders and thus have the potential to provide an alternative to the traditional gerontocracy of these areas, often in the past restricted to the eldership of the churches.

One question which this book has not yet addressed is one commonly asked of people who interest themselves in the Gaelic language – or indeed in small-scale peripheral communities. Why bother with any of that? What importance is it in the modern world? We are now into the arena of values and opinions. Any such debate deserves to be informed by the facts of history and the results of research. In attempting to learn the language of my great-grand-parents I was accused of looking back into the past and wasting my time 'because they all speak English anyway'. (Such arguments were not used about the Latin which I had to do at school.) Within the Gaelic communities Gaelic people actually said to me, 'It has no commercial value.' And, 'It won't buy you a pound of sausages once you cross the Minch!' The comments all betrayed an instrumental attitude, as if the functions of language were restricted to the transmission of factual information and the transaction of commerce.

The Gaelic speech-community is now almost entirely bilingual. In that fact Gaelic speakers have actually joined the majority of humankind – three-quarters of whom are bilingual. It is thus the predominant condition of the world's peoples. Monolingualism is typically the characteristic of dominant ethnic groups in a relatively few large-scale mass-societies. It is the result of forcing one's language upon subject peoples and requiring others to learn and use one's own language without bothering to learn theirs.

These imperialistic attitudes from the past are having to be quickly modified in today's world. Even in the United States, the largest of the 'monolingual mass-societies', non-English mother-tongue speakers are fast becoming the majority in many areas. In the Soviet Union non-Russians will soon be the majority overall and ethnic-minority and language rights are being stridently asserted. In Europe the EC member-states cannot agree on a single administrative language, and its educational policy directives require member-states' schools to teach two other EC languages in addition to their own. Had they got away with one, it would have been English everywhere, and neither France nor Germany would put up with that. The United Kingdom has so far managed to get away with a requirement for just one other foreign language in its schools – pleading that so many of its schoolchildren have to cope with their own ethnic minority languages in addition to English (as if the U.K. were unique in that respect!) The minority languages of Europe may yet save its linguistic soul. Gaelic now takes its place amongst 33 others in the E.C. – spoken collectively by over 30 million fellow Europeans. They may be able to encourage different attitudes towards language and new policies for present-day realities.

Research in Wales has indicated that the highest levels of spoken and written English within the education system of England and Wales are to be found in the schools using Welsh as the principal teaching medium. The results in other subjects also indicate that children in these schools are at an advantage. Such is the popularity of Welsh-medium education today that there is even a Welsh-medium school in London. Research has also upheld the success of the bilingual project in the Western Isles – and Gaelic-medium schooling is now the fastest-developing aspect of Scottish education. In this perhaps some parents are demonstrating an instrumental attitude. Welsh and Gaelic do help children to 'get on'. But there must be more to it than that. These languages are the key to much more than buying sausages on whatever side of the Minch.

Languages have expressive functions and the minority languages are the key to cultures in every way as valid and as expressive of the human condition as the majority languages. Lose the language and the culture dies. Do we want a European Community of twelve standardised member-state cultures – or a community of a hundred nations and regions each with its own distinctive character? In such a political association no member-state, nation or region could dominate the others as England dominates the United Kingdom. In such a Europe there would be no argument that a minority language is any disability to acquiring any other language of wider communication. Quite the contrary. The countries of a single standard official language are those whose people have difficulty coping with other languages. England is very much an example of that.

Language has a normative function too – in social control. The standardised languages of power deny any other alternative windows on the world – as did the Newspeak of Orwell's *1984*. The distinctive idiom of Gaelic and the different ways in which it expresses meaning compared with English and other European languages present an alternative understanding of reality. For Burns 'freedom and whisky gang thegither' – so too do freedom and Gaelic.

Above all, languages have a symbolic or social solidarity function in which feelings of togetherness can be celebrated. It is very difficult for speakers of a mass-language of wider communication to understand this – especially if their language has lost its distinctive dialects and accents. Their language enables them to gain access to world markets, the products of a world-wide entertainments industry and to international scholarship and learning. But this is no less true for bilingual minority-language speakers.

Monolingual majority-language speakers have lost their own language of solidarity and social reciprocity. They find it difficult to develop an alternative social and linguistic identity of their very own. They have only the one, and that they must share with others. A recent study of mother-tongue in our society quoted an Urdu speaker: 'There isn't another language which is part of the experience of the English native speaker, and that's where the problem lies.' (Wells, 1987) At least in Gaelic Scotland that is not the case – and perhaps from our 'peripheries' a solution may start to be found.

If bilingualism is such a good thing for indigenous and ethnic minority children, why should this benefit not be extended to all? If educational policy is serious in enabling all schoolchildren to acquire a second language, it is really futile to leave it to the secondary stage. The contrasting examples of Gaelic and French in our education system should indicate that teaching a language merely as a subject at the secondary stage does nothing to secure real fluency. Scotland could really lead the way if it is required to produce a 'national curriculum', by extending bilingual education to all by providing facilities for initial education through the mother-tongue (whether English, Gaelic, an ethnic minority or another European language) and at the same time enabling children effectively to acquire another of these as a second language in addition to their own. It could not be done overnight but it could be planned as an extension of what already exists – and it is not so different from what happens in many other countries poorer in resources than our own.

I entitled the final chapter of *The Lion's Tongue* 'A Gaelic Future', for I felt there would be one. In retrospect, the experience of the past sixteen years on the 'Gaelic Front' is greatly encouraging, for so many of the ideas mooted at that time have been implemented in some form or other. Moreover, some objective assessment of success has often followed their implementation, and I feel that there is some cause for continued if guarded optimism. It would be foolish to greet any of these developments or any assessment of them with euphoria. None of them in itself will bring in the Gaelic Millennium. But taken together and used actively as part of a concerted strategy, they could provide a future for a Gaelic community in the 21st Century. That chapter's conclusion can be repeated, I believe with greater confidence, sixteen years on: 'The Highland community which still remains in the Islands and the Northwest could still by girding itself together politically, by standing firm and by using its Gaelic as a weapon, develop a way of life in this modern world which was ecologically sound, capable of withstanding social or moral collapse of mainstream society should that occur, cherishing the land and its resources, promoting a satisfying culture for its people and again providing the world with a further example of successful response to adversity.'

APPENDIX: RESULTS OF 1981 SCOTTISH OPINION ON GAELIC SURVEY

Questions on Gaelic Policies (1981 Public Opinion Survey)

	% of whole sample with the question	% agreeing eliminating 'don't knows'
1. Do you think that the Gaelic language is important for the Scottish people as a whole?	41.2	49.8
2. Do you think that Gaelic should be officially recognised in Scotland?	54.2	66.7
3. Should more public money be available to encourage Gaelic?	45.9	54.7
4. Should Gaelic speakers be allowed to use Gaelic when dealing with public authorities?	41.2	57.0
5. Should more Gaelic speakers be appointed to public posts in Gaelic areas?	43.0	76.4
6. Do you think that Gaelic should be encouraged in the Highlands and Islands only?	27.3	35.8
or in Scotland as a whole?	49.0	64.2
7. Should children in any part of Scotland be able to learn Gaelic at school if they or their parents want it?	70.0	81.8
8. Would you yourself welcome more opportunities for adult education in Gaelic?	24.4	36.7
9. Should there be more radio and television programmes for Gaelic learners?	47.3	70.9
10. Have you ever seen or heard a Gaelic radio or television programme?	81.6	87.0
11. How much Gaelic do you think there should be on radio and television? Agreeing more/much more:	39.3	48.9
12. Have you ever noticed any Gaelic in newspapers and magazines?	11.9	14.0
13. Would you like to see the press give more encouragement to Gaelic?	31.5	68.4
14. How would you feel if you saw Gaelic used along with English on public signs, notices or adverts? In favour:	42.2	68.3
15. What is your own knowledge of Gaelic? Adequate to fluent/native speaker:	1.73	1.78
16. Have any members of your family been able to speak Gaelic? Yes:	14.7	15.2

BIBLIOGRAPHY

A: Gaelic Origins and Scottish History
BANNERMAN, J., *Studies in the History of Dalriada* (Edinburgh, Scottish Academic Press, 1974)
CAMERON, A. D., *Go Listen to the Crofters*: the Napier Commission and Crofting a Century Ago (Stornoway, Acair, 1986)
CHADWICK, H. M., *Early Scotland* (Cambridge, 1949)
DURKACZ, V. E., *The Decline of the Celtic Languages* (Edinburgh, John Donald, 1983)
GILLIES, W., (ed.) *Gaelic and Scotland Alba agus a' Ghàidhlig* (Edinburgh, University Press, 1989)
GRANT, I. F., *The Social and Economic Development of Scotland before 1603* (Edinburgh, Oliver & Boyd, 1930)
GRIGOR, I. F., *Mightier Than a Lord, the Highland Crofters' Struggle for the Land* (Stornoway, Acair, 1979)
HUNTER, J., *The Making of the Crofting Community* (Edinburgh, John Donald, 1976)
KERMACK, W. R., *The Scottish Highlands – a Short History (c.300-1746)* (Edinburgh, W & A.K. Johnston, 1957)
WITHERS, C.W.J., *Gaelic in Scotland 1698-1981: The Geographical History of a Language* (Edinburgh, John Donald, 1984)
WITHERS, C.W.J., *Gaelic Scotland – the Transformation of a Culture Region* (London, Routledge, 1988)

B: The Social Setting of Present-Day Gaelic Scotland
CHAPMAN, M., *The Gaelic Vision in Scottish Culture* (London, Croom Helm, 1978)
DARLING, F. F., *West Highland Survey* (London, 1955)
DORIAN, N. C., *The valuation of Gaelic by Different Mother Tongue Groups Resident in the Highlands*, Scottish Gaelic Studies, Vol. XIII, Pt. II, pp. 169-182, 1981)

DORIAN, N. C., *Language Death, The Life Cycle of a Scottish Gaelic Dialect* (Philadelphia, University of Philadelphia Press, 1981)

GRIMBLE, I., and THOMSON, D. S., (eds.) *The Future of the Highland* (London, Routledge, 1968)

HULBERT, J. (ed.) *Gaelic: Looking to the Future* (Longforgan, Dundee, Andrew Fletcher Society, 1985)

MACDONALD, M., *Cor na Gàidhlig — Language, Community and Development: the Gaelic Situation, a report...with recommendations for action* (Inverness, Highlands and Islands Development Board, 1982)

MacKINNON, K., *Gaelic in Scotland 1971: Some Sociological and Demographic Considerations of the Census Report for Gaelic* (Hatfield, Hertis Publications, 1978)

MacKINNON, K., *Gaelic in Highland Region — the 1981 Census* (Inverness, An Comunn Gàidhealach, 1984)

MacKINNON, K., *Gaelic Language Regeneration Amongst Young People in Scotland 1971-1981 From Census Data* (Hatfield, Hertis Publications, 1984)

MacKINNON, K., 'The Scottish Gaelic Speech-Community — Some Social Perspectives', plenary paper given at the First International Conference on the Languages of Scotland (Aberdeen University. Hatfield, Hertis Publications), and in *Scottish Language* No. 5 (Winter 1986) pp. 65-84,(1985)

MacKINNON, K., 'Gender, Occupational and Educational Factors in Gaelic Language-Shift and Regeneration' (paper to Third International Minority Languages Conference, University College of Galway, 20-26 June 1986) (Hatfield, Hertis Publications) and in Mac EOIN, G., Ahlqvist. A., and ó hAodha, D., (eds.) *Third International Conference on Minority Languages, Celtic Papers*, Clevedon, Multilingual Matters,(1986)

MacKINNON, K., 'Language Retreat and Regeneration in the Present-Day Scottish Gàidhealtachd' (paper to the First International Seminar on Geolinguistics, North Staffordshire Polytechnic, Stoke-on-Trent, 13-15 May 1987) forthcoming in: WILLIAMS, C. *Language, Territory and Community* (Clevedon, Multilingual Matters, 1987)

MacKINNON, K., 'Occupation, Migration and Language-Maintenance in Gaelic Communities' (paper to 9th International Seminar on Marginal Regions, Skye 5-11 June 1987) (Hatfield, Hertis Publications, 1987)

MacKINNON, K. & MacDONALD, M. *Ethnic communities: The Transmission of Language and Culture in Harris and Barra* (Report to the Social Science Research Council) (Hatfield, Hertis Publications, 1980)

MacLEAN, M., & CARRELL, C., (eds.) *As an Fhearann/From the Land — a Century of Images of the Scottish Highlands* (Edinburgh, Mainstream Publishing, 1986)

PRATTIS, J. I., *'Industrialisation and Minority-Language Loyalty: the Example of Lewis'*, chapter 3 in HAUGEN,E., McCLURE, J. D., and THOMSON, D. S., (1980) *Minority Languages Today*, a selection from the papers read at the First International Conference on Minority Languages held at Glasgow University from 8 to 13 September 1980, (Edinburgh, University Press, 1980)

VALLEE, F. G Social Structure and Organisation in a Hebridean Community: *A Study of Social Change*, Unpublished Ph. D. thesis, University of London,(1954)

C: Gaelic Language and Linguistics

CLEMENT, R. D., : Gaelic, ch. 20 in TRUDGILL, P. (ed.) (1984) *Language in the British Isles* (Cambridge, University Press,(1984)

GLEASURE, J.W. *'Gaelic: dialects, principal divisions' (pp.91-95)* in THOMSON, D.S., (ed.) (1983) The Companion to Gaelic Scotland (Oxford, Blackwell, 1983)

MacAULAY, D., *'Intra-dialectal variation as an area of Gaelic linguistic research'*, in *Scottish Gaelic Studies*, Vol. XIII, Pt.I., pp.81-97,(1978)

MacAULAY, D., *Borrow, calque and switch: the law of the English frontier'*, in ANDERSON,J. (ed.) *Language Form and Linguistic Variation* (Amsterdam, Benjamins, 1982)

D: Gaelic Literature, Culture, Music and the Arts

CAMPBELL, J. L. and COLLINSON, F. *Hebridean Folksongs, Vols, I/II/III* (London, Routledge, 1969)

MacLEOD, F., *Gaelic Arts, a Way Ahead*, a report for the Scottish Arts Council (Edinburgh, Scottish Arts Council, 1986)

THOMSON, D. S., *The Companion to Gaelic Scotland* (Oxford, Blackwell, 1983)

E: Gaelic in Education

MacKINNON, K., *Language, Education and Social Processes in a Gaelic Community* (London, Routledge, 1977)

MacKINNON, K., *The Present Position of Gaelic in Scottish Primary Education (Leeuwarden, Fryske Akademy/EMU-Projekt*, Hatfield: Hertis Publications,(1988)

MITCHELL, R., McINTYRE,D., MacDONALD, M., & McLENNAN, S., *Report of an Independent Evaluation of the Western Isles Bilingual Education Project* (University of Stirling, Department of Education, 1987)

MULHOLLAND, G., *The Struggle for a Language — Gaelic in Education* (Farr, Rank and File, 1980)

MURRAY, M. and MORRISON, C., *Bilingual Primary Education in the Western Isles, Scotland, Report of the Bilingual Education Project 1975-81* (Stornoway, Acair, 1984)